VOICE:

PSYCHE AND SOMA

VOICE:
PSYCHE AND SOMA

By CORNELIUS L. REID

THE JOSEPH PATELSON *MUSIC HOUSE*

NEW YORK

✓ MT
820
. R 368

International Standard Book Number: 0-915282-00-3
Library of Congress Card Number: 74-30987

Printed in the United States of America
Joseph Patelson Music House
160 West 56th Street, New York, N. Y. 10019

TO

WANDA

Man's choices will be 'judged'
by Nature, thus revealing the wisdom
of his selections from among many alternatives.
JONAS SALK

Acknowledgments

The sections "Core or Periphery" (Chapter I), "Stimulation of Involuntary Muscles" (Appendix I), and "Functional Studies" (Appendix III), originally appeared in an article called "Functional Vocal Training" published by *The Journal of Orgonomy*. Through the kind permission of Dr. Elsworth F. Baker, Editor, these sections have been included in this book.

The Author

TABLE OF CONTENTS

VOICE:
PSYCHE AND SOMA

PREFACE

FUNCTIONAL vocal training is founded on the belief that a correct technique must be an extension of free organic movement; that such movement is the expression of a life process subject to nature's laws; and that training procedures adopted must be based upon principles which conform to those laws. This premise is not widely accepted, most training methods preferring to concentrate on functional effects, rather than functional causes. This error has led to another misjudgment, even more serious: confusing the *process* of learning to sing with the *art of singing*. Procedures designed to restructure a faulty vocal technique, therefore, cannot have validity until a clear distinction is made between art, aesthetics and function.

Aesthetics is a philosophy dealing with beauty, its primary concern being the qualitative properties of a work of art. Art differs in that it is related to the use of skill and imagination in the production of things of beauty. Function is the natural action characteristic of a mechanical or organic system. Within a physical context, function is suitably described as natural or unatural, healthy or unhealthy, well-coordinated or awkward, blocked or free. Inasmuch as the vocal cords and the larynx itself must be positioned during phonation to meet specific tonal requirements, how these muscles adjust (function) is of paramount importance if the voice is to be well produced and free of muscular interference. Correct muscular coordination is synonymous with correct technique and makes the art of singing possible.

By the very nature of things, the average pupil presenting himself for study is more directly concerned with problems related to function than either art or aesthetics. His need is to correct technical faults which inhibit artistic expression, and rather drastic changes must be made in the muscular coordination involved in phonation if this is to be accomplished. For this reason the art of singing for a considerable period of time must be subordinated to functional needs. Inevitably, such constructions are often at variance with both art and aesthetics. A valid approach to training, therefore, must recognize a distinction between function as it relates to process, and the end result of that process as it is made to serve an artistic ideal.

The process of restructuring the vocal function involves three principal areas of interest: 1) the formation of correct concepts related to quality, 2) the mechanics of registration, and 3) the dynamic processes involved in natural movement. How existing concepts are bypassed and reformed, how the mechanics of registration are put into effect, and how natural movement is encouraged are functional aspects of training which will here receive attention. Suffice it to say that these are the elements upon which a secure vocal technique is founded. Without a functionally correct technique the use of skill and imagination, as well as matters pertaining to aesthetics, is of little consequence.

Since, as is unquestionably true, all important vocal muscles respond involuntarily and operate below the conscious level, very special techniques must be developed in order to bring involuntary responses under volitional control. This presents a unique problem, for, as long as the mechanism is impeded in its function by muscular interference, the singer cannot possibly know how to energize those elements of the phonative process upon which free tonal emission depends. Since the student is incapable of effectively acting upon his voice without first knowing how it should be acted upon (nor can he be meaningfully instructed to do so), training methods based upon direct control must, therefore, be discarded as worthless. Indeed, in all essentials, verbalization is virtually unnecessary. It is for this reason that the procedures advocated throughout these pages, and the principles subscribed to, reflect the influence of an earlier period—that of the first Golden Age of Singing.

Reputable scientific investigators are unanimously agreed upon one thing concerning the voice—no anatomical difference is to be found between the physical makeup of the gifted singer and the non-singer. That is to say, those who sing well hold no physiological advantage over those who cannot sing, or do not sing well. This forces the acceptance of but one conclusion— skill in singing depends upon physical coordination, upon a precisely adjusted laryngeal musculature. The 'gifts' are musicality, an ability to develop sharp tonal concepts, a sense of poesy and drama, imagination and personal charisma. When exposed to training procedures which bring the vocal function into harmony with nature's laws, those who possess these gifts should become outstanding singers.

C. L. R.

INTRODUCTION

A THOUGHTFUL study of vocal technique must deal with extremely complex issues. The singer's vocal mechanism is his own body and, quite literally, the act of vocalization is accomplished by transforming the respiratory system into a musical instrument. Singing, therefore, involves the whole person, with all of the usual conflicts and seeming contradictions. The entity which emerges as 'voice' is thus a composite of many influences—physical coordination, mental concepts, temperament, and psychological attitudes. The singer who has 'put it together' has succeeded in combining all of these factors in such a way as to have each contributing element complement the other.

It was Manuel Garcia who once said, 'All control over the tone is lost once the vocal cords become vibratile.'* This statement reflects a profound insight into the vocal process, as it categorically eliminates metaphysical concepts and recognizes 'voice' to be what it truly is: movements of the vocal cords which set the

---

*A parallel to this is observable in sports where all control over the ball is lost once it has left the racquet, club or bat. Control instituted after the cords have become vibratile is rarely helpful and, at best, only superficially so.

1

surrounding air spaces in motion. The mechanism responsible
for 'voice,' then, is the muscular system whose terminating point
is the vocal cords housed in the laryngeal pharynx. Tone, in
short, is the end result of a functional process and its quality and
character are largely determined by the efficiency with which the
muscles of the laryngeal pharynx respond. To ensure good tone
quality, training procedures must be put into effect which will
change and improve the way the vocal muscles are positioned
and held in tension.

On the basis of this premise it is apparent that one does not
train the 'voice' but rather the muscular system which produces
vibrations. That the movement potential of this system is subject
to specific functional laws goes without saying, and these will be
discussed at some length in the section devoted to the mechanics
of the vocal registers. Faulty coordination is the physical cause
of all vócal problems and the goal of vocal pedagogy is to develop
techniques which will recondition a badly conditioned reflex, i. e.,
recoordinate the muscular interplay within the laryngeal pharynx.
This is not as difficult as it seems, as the involuntary musculature
of the larynx can be made to respond reflexively through the use
of specifically arranged patterns of pitch, intensity and the vowel.

Numerous methods have been devised over the years to deal
with problems relating to vocal control, as succeeding generations
of teachers have groped for a practical solution. With the exception of those techniques developed during the eighteenth and nineteenth centuries none have been notably successful, most being concerned with peripheral matters (such as breathing techniques, the
fixing of tongue and mouth positions, etc., and sensations of vibration). To feel the tone in the masque, 'forward,' or at some point
at the top of the head as many suggest involves no functional
principle and offers nothing constructive to the training program.
Specific symptoms of vibration are the result, not the cause, of
muscular movement and the right 'feel' of the tone can only be
experienced after the physical adjustment which gave rise to that
sensation has first been made.

In recent years the subject has attracted the interest of many qualified scientists, with somewhat mixed results. At best, the investigations have opened up the possibility for sensible theorizing, while pulling the rug out from under those who cherish what is mistakenly believed to be 'traditional' practices, proving that 'breath control,' 'voice placement,' and nasal resonance are without validity. This adds up to a sizable plus, as it is now possible to develop an instructional program thoroughly grounded in functional principles which are both coherent and in relative agreement with other intellectual disciplines. But the obvious difficulty, how such knowledge is to be applied to practical teaching, has been avoided.

The four principle areas related to voice scrutinized by scientific investigators are: 1) acoustics, 2) anatomy, 3) physics, and 4) physiology. Each of these has contributed importantly to our present knowledge concerning the number and origin of the vocal registers as well as yielding other important factual data. The present book attempts to incorporate the fruit of these investigations in a way both practical and useful to everyday teaching. Yet the value of these studies must not be overestimated. One can know a great deal 'of' and 'about' the mechanics of voice without comprehending the significance of the functional process in the slightest.

Far more important than scientific data is an intuitive understanding of what singing is all about, and the essence of singing cannot be measured by Sonagrams, Fastax camera sequences, Tomographs, oscilloscopes, or X-ray techniques. These are analytical, not creative processes. What is germane to the real problem is a quality of empathy, combined with the ability to recognize many types of tonal textures and to equate each with the stimulus pattern to which it corresponds, as well as the knowledge of how to work through character structures which bind the student and impede his progress.

A comprehensive training program must place each of these phases in proper perspective. To a degree, it is not very difficult to recognize a logical correspondence between a tone quality which has appeared spontaneously and the stimulus (the physical makeup

of a given scale pattern, i. e., a particular set of arrangements
utilizing pitch, intensity and the vowel) which prompted the response. To discover these parallels one need only observe and,
while observing, set aside personal prejudices and emotional attitudes which preclude objective learning.

Before the era of scientific investigation many notable teachers
(Tosi, Mancini, the Lampertis and Garcia, to name but a few)
recognized definite parallels between stimulus and response and
promulgated a theory of registration which remains valid to the
present. These parallels will subsequently be demonstrated and
justified physiologically. What will be pointed out is the existence
of a positive correlation between pitch, intensity and the vowel,
and the length, gauge and tension of the vocal cords. As a result,
the unique tonal textures yielded by the vocal registers (now
mistakenly attributed to resonance in the chest and head cavities)
can be properly identified with their functional origins. These
correlatives are crucial to an understanding of 'voice,' and, when
recognized, permit training procedures to be established on a
practical basis.

The limiting factor in such a discussion, of course, is that tone
qualities cannot be adequately described. To circumvent this
difficulty a vocal terminology will be adopted which, while loose
and somewhat arbitrary, is nevertheless recognizable by most
singers and teachers of singing. All metaphysical concepts have
been discarded, with functional matters being dealt with in functional terms. Considerable attention is given, perhaps for the first
time, to the significance of movement, especially the significance
of internal organic movement and its relationship to emotion.
Despite all of the difficulties involved, one fact should clearly
emerge: the vocal mechanism *is* accessible, and it *is* possible to
restructure a faulty technique without recourse to either poetic
musings or methods of direct control.

CHAPTER I

MUSCLES and MOVEMENT

THE ACT of phonation is accomplished by transforming the respiratory tract into a musical instrument, the act itself involving a positive movement from relaxation to balanced tension. Two basic functional events occur at this time: 1) the muscular contractions which position the vocal cords to make possible the numerous combinations of pitch, intensity and the vowel, and 2) the movement of those muscles which position the larynx so as to enable it to act efficiently as a primary resonator.

The muscular adjustments made in order to hold the cords in tension and position the larynx are, apart from the quality of the concepts which stimulate them, the essential activity which determines whether or not the vocal technique is functionally efficient. With this consideration in mind it might be helpful to comment briefly on some of the more important properties of muscular movement and define them. These properties are equilibrium, tonicity, tension and relaxation.

5

EQUILIBRIUM

THE BODY is so arranged that the muscles attached to the skeletal framework are paired in the manner of a complex system of pulleys. Thus, for every action made possible by one set of muscular contractions a counter movement can be made because of the contraction of other muscle groups which perform as natural antagonists. With the body so made up of an opposed muscular system of great intricacy, innumerable possibilities exist for physical participation ranging from the awkward to the graceful, the ineffectual to the harmonious.

Economy of movement is achieved when during a given act those muscles which have nothing positive to contribute to its execution remain passive, while those which should bear the burden of effort become active. When muscles which should be passive become active they interfere, causing the mechanism to become tense. Regardless of the quality of the response made, however, the response itself is the coordinative process. To be well coordinated, physically or vocally, is to be free of muscular interference.

The muscular complex engaged in phonation is in equilibrium when all of the muscle groups involved are in correct balance. For example, the muscles which stretch the vocal cords are in equilibrium when the ratio of tension shared between them is correct. Other examples worth citing are the breathing muscles having control over the inspiratory and expiratory processes. These include the three layers of abdominal muscles extending from the pelvis to the lower ribs; the diaphragm, which descends with each intake of breath and moves the rib cage outward; the suspensory muscles responsible for positioning the larynx; and the muscles within the pharyngeal tract which influence the vocal resonators, as well as those governing the articulatory processes, the tongue, jaw and palatal muscles in particular. A correct technique of singing finds these processes in equilibrium not only with themselves, but with each other.

TONICITY

W HEREAS coordination refers to the character of the response supplied by the muscular system in terms of interference or non-interference, and equilibrium to precision and rightness of balance, tonicity refers to the condition of the muscles as they stand ready to move in response to an appropriate stimulus.

The body is said to be in a high state of tone when the muscular system responds rapidly, in a low state of tone when it responds sluggishly. The correlation between the nervous system and muscle tone is obvious, but it is only one aspect of tone. An athlete, for example, is in good condition when his body is in a good state of 'tone,' indicating that the muscles are not only well coordinated but strong and without flabbiness. Young singers with dramatic potential must take this into consideration and resist the temptation of singing heavy roles until physical maturation has taken place. No singer before the age of thirty-five has had time to build up the tonicity necessary to surmount the difficulties of heavy roles without subjecting the vocal organs to undue strain. It should also be clear that the purpose of training and the use of scales and exercises goes beyond effecting changes within the coordinative process; they must also be projected with the aim of bringing the muscles into a high state of tonicity.

TENSION AND RELAXATION

W HENEVER there is muscular movement there must be tension. Tension, therefore, plays an important role in the phonative process since muscular movement is necessary. Without tension there can be neither pitch nor tonal amplification. Tension is an integral part of the coordinative process, of equilibrium and tonus. The focal point of pedagogic interest is to influence and improve the coordinative process, to induce correct tension and eliminate wrong tension, so that the muscles of the laryngeal and pharyngeal tract work together harmoniously.

Relaxation becomes a positive aspect of instruction only to the extent that it implies, 'Stop! All effort is being misdirected, so do nothing!' To relax is, quite literally, to 'do nothing.' It is good advice to the extent that it helps the student assume a proper attitude of readiness. Relaxation is merely a preliminary condition of being, one which is essential to free response but not part of the response itself. Correct affirmative action, i. e., tension within the coordinative process without tenseness, is the cause of the apparent relaxation and ease of execution so common to great singers. Tension must not be confused with tenseness; they are two different things. Legitimate tension is initiated through rhythmic movement and is essential to correct vocalization.*

RHYTHM—MOVEMENT—TECHNIQUE

IF MOVEMENT ceased, the universe would no longer exist, for in nature there is an ongoing ontology—rhythm, if you like. The galaxies are in a constant state of expansion and contraction, civilizations rise and fall, the seasons change, cells expand, contract, divide and proliferate, and life forms have their cycles, all phenomena being expressed in terms of ebb and flow —in terms of movement, rhythm. Movement is characteristic of all animate nature and reflects the manner in which energy is being expended. It is the mode through which contact is made with our inner being, our fellow humans, and the universe at large.

As part of our own nature, as well as nature at large, the vocal organs, too, move rhythmically in accordance with their own logic. The purpose of technical study, therefore, is to apply functional principles which will bring the vocal muscles into equilibrium,

---

*Even when dealing with psychological tension the advice to relax is largely useless, as the singer is being asked to release the very fears and anxieties which had initiated the tensions in the first place. To a considerable degree, however, tensions growing out of anxiety can be alleviated by proper vocal development, through the mechanics of registration.

develop a high state of muscle tone, and, through rhythmic movement, eliminate wrong tension and refine concepts. Once a freer
response to a rhythmic impetus occurs, the mechanism will of
itself clearly indicate how it prefers to readjust—an inner impetus
prompting it to move *this* way and not *that* way. At this juncture
the student's latent talent will surface and his intuitive 'feel' for
singing incline him to do that which is functionally correct. Were
it not possible to stimulate natural movement, all hope of reco-
ordinating an involuntary muscular system, or rechanneling misdirected energy, would have to be abandoned.*

---

*See: Appendix I for techniques useful to the proper stimulation of invol-
untary muscles.

*In the long run, methods devised to stimulate natural move-
ment through rhythmic identification supersede all other theoretical
considerations. Without such procedures technical improvement is
impossible.*

ENERGY—NATURAL MOVEMENT—ANXIETY

A GREAT DEAL is presently known about the
activity of the respiratory (vocal) muscles during phonation—
how they move, what type of adjustments are likely to be associated with certain kinds of tone quality, as well as the pitch and
intensity levels to which the various adjustments correspond. But
these are physiological considerations, expressed without reference
to the psychological factors involved. Little has been said about
the ability of these muscles to move, i. e., their freedom to do so
or the lack of it. Nor has much thought been given to the effect
of psychic tensions on the singer's movement potential.

The ability of a muscle to move, or natural movement, is conditioned by two factors: 1) a sense of physical coordination, and
2) emotion. Physically, 'having a voice' is an act of muscular
coordination which takes place as the respiratory organs adapt
to the vocal process. Musicality is not necessarily a prerequisite,
and it is paradoxical that the ability to produce beautiful tone

quality is in some instances virtually extracted from tonal thinking. Of the two, the physical and the conceptual, it is often difficult to determine which has acted as the catalyst. Regardless of concepts, however, the singer is constrained to deal with that type of tone quality which the physical condition of his voice, i. e., the coordinative process, yields at a particular moment.

An ability to identify satisfactorily with the phonative process on an emotional level is perhaps more important than a gift for physical coordination. It plays a prominent role in determining the type of tone quality to which the singer finds himself instinctively drawn, as well as being reflected in physical attitudes. Emotion means to 'move out,' and one's ability to move freely and spontaneously is predicated upon an absence of physical blockages brought on by emotional tension. Regardless of the rightness of the functional principles being applied, movement potential will inevitably be inhibited by psychological tension.

*The inevitable consequence of psychological tension is an inhibition of respiration.** Biologically, inhibited respiration performs the function of reducing the production of energy in the organism. The reason for this is clear. If a smaller amount of energy is created the motor impulses generated will be less intense and, as a result, easier to deal with. Thus, the reduction of energy output also results in the reduction of anxiety. Since inhibition of respiration is the psychological mechanism for suppressing anxiety and repressing feeling, the singer experiences difficulty in energizing

---

*Without oxygen there can be neither combustion nor production of energy. Heat and kinetic energy depend upon oxygen, and a free exchange of oxygen for carbon dioxide is essential to healthy organic life. Energy output, therefore, can be diminished by reducing the amount of oxygen introduced into the system. Thus, through shallow respiration, intensity of feeling will be lowered and, correspondingly, anxiety. Since emotional intensity is held at tolerable levels by regulating the respiratory process, the breathing mechanism may be seen to be the somatic counterpart of emotional repression and psychological factors synonymous with energy. To be effective, training procedures must confront this problem, as a correct technique of singing depends upon kinetic energy which has been built up and released, not suppressed. The principles governing registration are extremely useful in this connection, since they vitalize the muscles, release feeling, and promote spontaneous movement.

his voice properly, as well as in relating to the emotional content of the music. As a consequence, he finds himself unable to move spontaneously and fails to adapt easily to the vocal process.

The obvious correlation between inhibited body movement and psychological attitudes bears further comment. Since the beginning, man has erected defense mechanisms to protect himself from a fear of his own sensations. As a result, he became 'armored.' Elsworth F. Baker defines two kinds of armoring, 'natural or temporary muscular contractions and permanent or chronic contraction.' He then says, 'the former occurs in any living animal when it is threatened, but is given up when the threat is no longer present. . . .' The latter originates in the same manner, but because of continued threats is maintained and becomes chronic, reacting eventually to permanent inner rather than environmental dangers . . . (1). Of particular interest is the fact that armoring is known to divide into seven segments (ocular, oral, cervical, thoracic, diaphragmatic, abdominal, and pelvic), and that each of these segments, except the ocular, forms an integral part of the respiratory (vocal) system. The unrelieved muscular tension associated with armoring further complicates an already complicated vocal problem.

While it does seem hazardous to generalize in such matters, it is nevertheless apparent that singers fall into two broad psychological categories—three, if we recognize the compulsive singer who seems bent on destroying his vocal resources. First, there are those who control their anger through repression, by means of muscular armoring; and second, those who are able to break through one or more layers of restrictive tension and find release for their hostility and aggression through positive action. Of the two, the latter are far easier to train. Those who direct their anger outwardly do release their feelings; they are less inhibited and, consequently, able to function more effectively. This view is partially substantiated by observing the performance level found acceptable at the present time. The majority of successful singers appear to belong in the second category and reveal a singing style which, while limited and rather one dimensional on an emotional level, nevertheless possesses an aggressive quality that projects a certain vitality across the footlights.

Anxious singers who repress their feelings are a special problem. Not only do they resist, but the suppression of their anxiety is accomplished by bringing the swallowing muscles into tension, which inadvertently constricts the throat. Even when forcing themselves as an act of will to be more aggressive, those falling within this category find it difficult to relinquish the safe hold they maintain on their throats and feelings, and the use of greater energy is often counter productive; the more vigorously they work to open up, the harder the constrictor muscles tend to resist. This is not to say, however, that the resistances peculiar to either of the types described cannot be broken down. With time and patience a more open-throated resonance can be achieved, in which case the singer will gain on two levels: he will have freed his voice and freed himself of many psychological inhibitions.

A possible explanation for the contradiction in behavior between the two broad types described is this: those who suppress their anxiety by minimizing the ebb and flow of natural respiration cause the dammed up energy to move into the internal organs where it is bottled up; whereas those less armored are able to release energy into the muscle system. From this it should be evident that the manner in which energy is utilized represents the qualitative factor in rhythmic sensitivity, in one's capacity to identify emotionally to a given stimulus, and in one's general capacity for motility. *Psychologically, singing is an aggressive act.* For one to 'open up,' energy must move into the muscles rather than turning inward.

If emotion is understood to be a process of bodily expansion, of moving out, it will then be clear that anxiety not only arrests organic motility, but inhibits healthy emotional expression as well. That this has an adverse effect upon the vocal process goes without saying, for whatever the degree of chronic muscular contraction brought on by anxiety, to that degree will the vocal process and respiration be impeded. Here, obviously, we come upon an aspect of interference having nothing to do with singing *per se*. For this reason, among those who are equally talented, some will forge ahead and progress while others will pull back, literally being forced to remain within the boundaries set by their psychic tensions. In sum, the fears underlying psychic tensions arouse a profound distrust of involuntary movement and thus act as a serious impediment to vocal progress.

'VOICE' AS PERSON

ANY PROGRAM designed to promote organic movement when such movement has been held in check will constitute a threat and arouse anxiety. The direct purpose of functional vocal training is to provoke such movements and, through the mechanics of registration, bring about fundamental changes within the coordinative process giving rise to 'voice.' The result is to upset both the physical and emotional equilibrium to which the student has become accustomed and which he has learned to accept as a legitimate part of the self. Participation in a program designed to bring about dynamic changes of this description is bound to undermine one's security, raising, as it does, one of the most agonizing of all questions, 'Who am I?' and 'Is the "I" I think myself to be truly me?' It is seeking the answer to this question which makes genuine vocal growth so challenging.

By viewing 'voice' as an extension of the person, it becomes apparent that 'growing up' vocally can be just as trying an experience as growing up physically and emotionally. Indeed, undergoing vocal training based upon functional needs is very much like passing through adolescence. There is the same feeling of being in limbo, of an absence of self-identification. This is the risk factor in emotional growth, and it is the risk factor in vocal growth. This being so, training procedures designed to improve function touch upon a very sensitive area, as correction of a vocal problem is equivalent to an attack on the student's emotional core.

Under these circumstances singing becomes a far more complicated procedure than one might have at first supposed. Restricted to purely physical dimensions there are but two factors to be considered, registration and resonance. But neither of these operates in a vacuum and must be considered part of the total person, with allowance made for judgments and attitudes toward creative goals, aesthetic concepts and ideals, physical potential, and emotional blockages. It is the latter which may now be seen to hamper progress so severely. Chronic muscular contraction within the respiratory tract brought on by anxiety arrests free movement, and this condition seriously impairs the muscular adjustments governing registration, as well as the action of the suspensory muscles which position the larynx. Vocal training, therefore, while directly concerned with registration and adjustments for resonance, must, through them, also break down tensions brought on by organic contraction due to anxiety.*

Solving vocal problems by applying techniques which encourage natural movement and cause interfering muscles to relinquish their hold can be painful. To feel free movement within a muscular system which over the years has to some extent been bound arouses the very fears, real or imagined, from which all of us spend so much time and energy trying to hide; fear of being exposed and vulnerable, fear of the unknown, fear of losing control, fear of the sensual pleasure aroused as a consequence of organic expansion, and, sometimes, fear of succeeding. Overcoming fears of this kind is essential to progress for they must be overcome if expansive movement is to replace the confining tensions to which the singer has become habituated. Expansive movement is anxiety provoking, but going with such movement is unavoidable if the student is to progress.

One of the disappointments of functional training is that many who study are incapable of crossing this Rubicon. A surprising number are hampered by a limited freedom tolerance and it is impossible to nudge them beyond a certain point, each move

---

*For a more extended treatment of psychic tensions and their effect upon the voice, see: The Voice of Neurosis, by Paul L. Moses, New York: Grune and Stratton, 1954.

toward functional freedom being resolutely countered by a new kind of blockage. The ingenuity with which this is accomplished is often quite startling, especially since the student's professed aim is to improve. One part of his nature may desire to be free, but physically, at the crucial moment, his anxiety will get the better of him. *Especially for the extremely talented, inner tensions are the single greatest obstacle to vocal development.*

The consequence of one's emotional constitution on phonation cannot be overestimated. Indeed, singing, or learning to sing, would seem to be impossible unless one is free of psychological tensions. Fortunately, such is not the case. Many highly neurotic individuals sing beautifully, just as many emotionally stable individuals cannot sing at all. In the first instance the singer has learned to make his neurosis work for him. Sublimation must be considered within this context, but more important perhaps is an inner longing for contact with others, as the desire to 'reach out' is, in a very real sense, a precursor of expansive movement. Furthermore, muscular armoring, which commonly centers in the throat, does not always settle in that area, but will often lodge in the pelvic region, the abdomen, or the diaphragm. When psychic tensions have not invaded the laryngeal area, singing as an aggressive act can have a certain freedom and drive since, under these circumstances, the laryngeal muscles would be able to operate at a high level of efficiency.) As for those who are emotionally stable, it is possible to be free of inner tensions without necessarily being an athlete, and the singer is a vocal athlete.

If one's characterological structure seems to make the training program more complicated, it does. Surely it is difficult enough to obtain volitional control over involuntary muscles when there are no psychological problems with which to contend without having to deal with emotional tenseness as well. To a remarkable degree, however, normal work on register development and adjustments for resonance will go a long way toward restoring lost motility, regardless of its origin. By stimulating movement within the laryngeal pharynx and relieving throat constriction, other tensions throughout the respiratory tract will 'let go', not always, of course, but often enough for efforts made in that direction to be justified. For the student who pursues this course there are two possible advantages: he will have learned how to sing correctly, and he will have grown into a deeper knowledge of himself as a person.

FUNCTIONAL LISTENING

IT SHOULD now be evident that retraining the vocal muscles involves more than a knowledge of vocal mechanics. One must deal with psychological resistances as well. But the process of correcting vocal errors involves yet another important activity: the 'ear' must be trained to hear functionally.

Learning to hear functionally means that one judges and evaluates tone qualities for their instrinsic health, and as a reflection of a coordinative process, rather than for any aesthetic value. Not every healthy sound yielded by the vocal organs is lovely, any more than all sounds judged to be agreeable to the hearing are functionally healthy. Purely aesthetic listening limits progress, as many qualities having little or no aesthetic value can often be extremely useful to the training program. Two such cases in point are the rather crude chest register sounds that sometimes appear in the initial stages of training when working with a badly co-ordinated female voice, and the male falsetto. Neither possesses aesthetic value, but each is important to the restructuring process.

Even more difficult than learning to hear functionally is the art of combining functional listening with empathetic listening, Empathetic listening finds the teacher literally 'tuned in,' kinetically, to the physical and psychological forces at work within the student. Functional listening, an understanding of the mechanics of registration, and empathetic listening are basic requirements for those who teach voice. Without them, technical progress will be left to chance.

The student's relationship to listening and hearing, while far more complex, starts with learning to hear functionally. In the hands of a competent teacher the two register mechanisms can be established with very little difficulty, and the student should be quick to recognize the parallels between a particular pitch, intensity and vowel pattern, and the tonal texture evoked. The art of being aware of sensations of vibration. Far more important representing as it does increasingly subtle refinements which tend to blur and obscure the register outlines. At this point the student must be encouraged to 'tune in' and gain the 'feel' of what is happening as well as discern the source of the influences at work. This is not to suggest that kinetic identification is solely a matter of being aware of sensations of vibrations. Far more important is a sense of yielding to the naturalness of inner organic movements and learning to enjoy the exhilaration and pleasure so much a part of correct vocalization. The origin of all sensations, however, lies with movement, and the interior movements of the mechanism are inseparable from registration.

QUALITY AND TEXTURE

IN DEVELOPING his voice the student must learn to make a somewhat arbitrary distinction between quality and texture. Quality is that property of tone, apart from pitch and intensity, which is determined by its harmonic structure, by the relationship between its overtones and the fundamental. Aesthetically, quality is thought of in terms of beauty, of that which either pleases or displeases the ear. Texture, on the contrary, is a particular kind of quality and defines its properties. Two singers, for instance, may have equally beautiful voices, yet have instruments of contrasting texture—one being dark and velvety, the other fine grained, or perhaps clear and brilliant.

There is, however, a third type of tonal texture to be considered, one having little to do with temperament, ethnic background, musicality or intrinsically 'natural' properties, but with registration.

To an ear sharply tuned to functional events there is in every tone the obvious presence of the falsetto and the chest register, a fact which gives to all voices of stature a certain similarity while, at the same time, preserving their uniqueness. The influence of registration on texture is, obviously, independent of individual peculiarities and solely the product of functional mechanics. An instrument provides a useful analogy. Several violinists playing the same instrument will draw forth different qualities and textures because of personal attributes, but the mechanical features, the quality identified with each of the strings, will remain much the same.

The distinction being made between texture and quality is important to the learning process and, indeed, to an understanding of vocal mechanics. Each voice possesses tonal properties which are intrinsically natural to the individual, his anatomical structure, his temperament, his musicality, and his sense of physical coordination. But, as with instruments, there is a particular kind of quality which belongs to the stringing, to a given area of pitch and intensity. With the voice, this is the product of registration and, hence, functionally oriented. Functional listening addresses itself to these textures, rather than to those which are the product of quality per se.

Registration, inner organic movement, and sensations of vibration are all aspects of function which, with concepts, combine to yield a specific kind of tone quality. Efforts to improve the technique, then, must be directed toward effecting meaningful changes within each of these separate, yet inseparable, areas. It is concepts which, because of the singer's desire to cling to what is known and familiar, most frequently stand in the way.

Those who hold rigidly to a fixed idea of quality are virtually unteachable. One cannot progress without change and, while all change is not progress, nevertheless one must remain flexible enough to risk a new experience and at least try new qualities on for size. Quality concepts normally constitute a problem for one reason: due to technical imperfections, the intrinsically natural quality of the singer's voice is the one quality neither the teacher nor the singer himself has yet heard. Quality, in brief, reflects the condition of the functioning mechanism. Faulty inner organic movements, incorrect sensations of vibration, and an imbalanced registration are normal to the average singer and distort his natural tone quality. Since it is registration which recoordinates the movement characteristics of the laryngeal musculature, which changes the character of the sensations of vibration experienced by the singer, and which helps position the larynx more precisely so as to bring about a functional improvement in the resonance characteristics, quality must be manipulated through the mechanics of registration. A fixed idea of quality prohibits necessary changes from taking place and limits progress. *Aural recognition of quality changes brought on by specifically arranged pitch-intensity patterns (registration) is the key to functional listening.* It is also essential to the development and refinement of concepts.

Functional listening avoids many of the pitfalls lying in wait for the unsuspecting. One of its greatest virtues is to skirt three seemingly insurmountable difficulties: 1) emotional listening, 2) faulty concepts, and 3) lack of objectivity.

The reason one artist is admired more than another, equally fine, often has to do with emotional hearing and helps explain why singers and teachers idealize a certain type of tone quality. Obviously, the sound one attempts to produce and the sound one admires in others satisfies some emotional need, or represents an emotional attitude; otherwise there would be an absence of self-identification. Hearing, therefore, and concepts themselves, have a characterological basis, and it is safe to say that emotional factors are strongly present in concepts related to self-listening and self-expression as well as aesthetic goals. For this reason learning to sing more correctly will refine one's sensitivity, alter aesthetic values, release a latent capacity for feeling and, by definition, retune the hearing process. At the same time, the fantasies so often associated with self-image will be replaced by a deepening self-awareness.

QUALITY, IMITATION AND SELF-LISTENING

THE NATURAL admiration one holds for an artist poses yet another problem. Anyone who sings as a youngster intuitively sets up his own idols, and quite rightly. One needs a model, one needs inspiration, and who can supply these better than a great singer? But, as with everything that pertains to the voice, there is a trap. To admire the sweetness and 'ring' of Bjoerling's voice is natural. Unfortunately, to imitate it is also natural. This marks the beginning of the singer's difficulties. Failing to ask the basic question, 'Why does my own voice not ring in similar fashion?' the singer proceeds to 'make' his tones vibrant and by so doing engages constrictor tensions. What he has failed to realize is this: a genuine ring in the voice is the product of correct function, right concepts and precise muscular coordination. The former can, at an appropriate time, be emulated; the latter must be learned.

To imitate a finished product when such faults as throatiness, nasality, breathiness, impure vowels, a limited tonal range, and a poor laryngeal suspension (the latter condition being reflected in tones described as 'unfocused') are present, serves no useful purpose. A serious mistake too often made is to avoid functional processes by striving for ultimate goals instead of immediate objectives. This is a serious miscalculation. Quality is the product of function and is purified by perfecting the interior muscular processes responsible for yielding tone. Constructive changes cannot be made except through the mechanics of registration and, if the voice is to improve, both quality and the concepts which influence physical responses must also change. Those who cannot discard their preconceived notions concerning idealized quality concepts stand in their own way, especially so since objective hearing is impossible.

Lack of objectivity further complicates this already complicated phase of the subject. Not being able to hear himself properly, having, at best, a shaky knowledge of functional mechanics, and with the sounds he produces always coming back to him in some-what distorted form, the student is ill-equipped, either by experience or circumstance, to make effective value judgments. Nor is his state of confusion eased by the often contradictory, if well meaning, advice so freely proferred from all sides. He must run a gauntlet as one blindfolded—being at the mercy of the taste, judgment, knowledge and psychological attitudes of his voice teacher, his coaches, his manager, his conductors, his accompanists, his confreres, his fellow students and his friends. The odds against survival, as indicated by the extremely high incidence of vocal decline and failure, are enough to discourage even the inveterate gambler.

PHYSICAL PROBLEMS

To THE ALREADY serious obstacles mentioned there must be added another: unsuspected physical impediments. In recent years a number of my students have discovered through chance x-rays having been taken that their spinal column, because of long forgotten accidents, was badly out of line. In an extreme case the nerve endings of one pupil failed to make contact with the larynx, with the result that her voice always sounded hoarse, especially after singing. Under medical supervision her posture improved, the jaw and head set assumed a more natural position, and she was for the first time able to sing without fatigue. A direct consequence of her physical improvement was that the hoarseness about which she had so long complained completely disappeared. One wonders how many there are whose problems are multiplied by correctable physical difficulties having no direct relationship to vocal technique per se. Obviously, when the spinal column is out of line the voice is not going to work properly. A thorough medical examination should, when such questions arise, relieve all doubt and uncertainty, as well as dictate the proper course of action to be taken.

QUALITY CONCEPTS

I T SHOULD now be evident that the student's path to success is not easy. A faulty vocal self image, the fact that sounds return to him in somewhat distorted form, his need to emulate, his natural inclination to imitate, his innate fear of inner expansion, the often worthless advice so freely proferred, the necessity of contending with physical problems not directly related to singing per se, and the almost impossible task of being both subjective and objective about his own sound, make the learning process extremely hazardous.

Above all other considerations, concepts related to quality are the hardest to reconcile. It is not easy to discard an aesthetic ideal and accept new sounds based upon functional mechanics. Neither the male falsetto nor the female chest register offers, in the beginning, tonal qualities which are very reassuring and to identify with them, even on a temporary basis, can be trying. This—combined with the fact that new sounds emerge, new sensations are experienced, and the newly awakened awareness of freer organic movement brings on a slight disorientation—makes for an understandable uncertainty. Every step along the way seems to present a calculated risk.

Quality, self-listening and imitation are tricky concepts and must be worked at through registration. By listening to and, in the beginning, imitating the textural properties belonging to each register mechanism, one avoids all misconcepts concerning 'my quality,' or 'making' what is thought to be resonance. In so doing the student will be able to follow a clear path. He will recognize the sounds belonging to a divided registration and, during the process of blending them, keep track of the textural balances as the two mechanisms merge into one. Making these changes through kinetic identification and functional listening refines one's aesthetic sensitivity and prepares the way for making the desired 'color' effects so essential to interpretation.

NATURAL SINGING

THE DEVELOPMENT of a beneficial method of vocal pedagogy depends in the long run upon the establishment of a value system which corresponds to, and agrees with, natural order. By natural order is meant those forces, known and unknown, which operate upon and within us and by which we are all bound. Concepts, the use of energy, emotion, hearing and listening, together with the positioning of the vocal muscles which occurs as the respiratory organs adapt to the vocal process, must all be in equilibrium if the vocal technique is to be natural and functioning freely. How to stimulate movement on the one hand, and how to get around inhibitions brought on by emotional tension on the other, is the central difficulty to be surmounted. If training is to be successful, the functional principles applied must encourage free, natural movement.

CORE OR PERIPHERY?

IN A RATHER whimsical moment, D. A. Clippenger wrote that the real art of singing was lost immediately after it was found . . . [that] the only time it was perfect was when it began . . . [and] ever since it began we have been searching for it without success (2). This statement seems ludicrous, but it is at the same time extremely perceptive. Man has always been at odds with his own nature, as well as the nature around him. We read in the Bible of man's need to be reborn, to rid himself of the old Adam and take on the new man, to become as a little child. Philosophies abound with the intent of showing the way back to a state of nature which has been lost.

The history of vocal training has followed this same pattern. Great teachers have had special insights into functional activities and have understood the mechanism. These special qualities were lost because they could not be passed on like family heirlooms, each successive generation of teachers having to rediscover that which had already been discovered. As in other areas of learning, new bodies of knowledge have through the years been incorporated which on the surface would seem to clarify training procedures and expedite progress. Unfortunately, the reverse is too often the case, the simple being rejected for the complex, the core for the periphery, the natural way for mechanistic methods. Too often man builds better mousetraps only to become caught in them.

The structure upon which early training practices relied was obviously one in which functional laws were formulated, understood, and utilized on a practical basis. Proof of this is to be found in a statement by Mancini (1716-1800) 'Art,' he suggests, 'consists of knowing where nature directs us, and to what we have been destined; understanding at once the gifts of nature, cultivating them easily, man can perfect himself; how sure is harvest for the attentive farmer, who has observed and understood the different seeds, which are fecund in diverse types of earth' (3). Another writer, Isaac Nathan (1792-1864), a legitimate heir of the Porpora school, made a distinction between core and periphery when he declared, 'The subject of voice includes two principle considerations, tone and articulation. . . . To the organs of tone, which will be briefly noticed in the progress of this treatise, the nose, the uvula, the palate, the teeth, and the lips, may be considered only as auxiliaries, since they are more especially organs of articulation . . .' (4).

If Mancini's analogy ·to farming is taken seriously, we can retrace our way to the point where functional health, resonance, vowel purity, and purity of intonation meet as one. For, without question, his statement indicates an awareness of function, of a correlation between stimulus and response, of the importance of gaining consonance with nature's laws and, by implication, that the organic response of the vocal mechanism is predictable.

It has already been indicated that registration is an organic response to a stimulus pattern comprised of pitch and intensity. If the vowel is considered, it, too, will be recognized as being the result of a positioning process. This process involves not only the vocal cords, but the entire respiratory system. When the system is well coordinated, the tone quality is pure. When there is muscular interference, there will be a corresponding degree of tonal distortion. Thus, the idea that has been projected as a conceptual image to which the student responds is similar to the planting of seed in the ground, while the vocal organs can be compared with the fertile earth. When the total environment is favorable to the needs of internal organs, a natural growth process takes place. Just as plant life flourishes when exposed to a congenial climate, so, also, the vocal mechanism will yield sounds which are pure, resonant, flexible, and capable of encompassing an extensive tonal range whenever they are confronted with the kind of environment their growth pattern demands. As long as this energy exchange is maintained in perfect balance, the voice will be free and totally responsive to the singer's will.

Purity of intonation and registration remained clear-cut concepts for almost three centuries. Judged on the basis of Mancini's observation, training procedures were purely functional. The Porpora school placed some emphasis on breathing, but the idea of breath 'control' was a much later development. Other and more serious departures were to follow. Garcia's invention of the laryngoscope was one. Another occurred toward the end of the nineteenth century. Singers who could best be described as having natural voices (voices extremely well formed with little or no formal training) introduced, when their careers had terminated and they became teachers, concepts which can only be described as pure fantasy. Lilli Lehmann (1848-1929) was a leading exponent of this kind of school, and her book contains entire chapters given over to the Resonance of the Head Cavities, Sensations of the Palate, Sensations of the Nose, and Sensations of the Tongue (5). The renowned Alessandro Bonci (1870-1945) brought this kind of thinking to its logical conclusion when he said, 'Singing is like squeezing paint out of a tube' (6).

The Lehmann-Bonci 'nonsense school' must be rejected out of hand as an unfortunate aberration having nothing to do with tradition or new bodies of learning. Far more serious has been another kind of misdirection. Herman Klein, a distinguished pupil of Garcia, one who collaborated in the preparation of *Hints on Singing,* offers a clear example of how well-intentioned friends and supporters can abandon the functional core for peripheral concerns. In Garcia's *Hints,* there are seven pages of material on the registers of the voice; not one word on resonance, very little on breathing, and nothing on breath 'control.'

Writing some years later, Klein lists the various elements of Garcia's training procedures in the order of their importance. These are set forth as follows: (a) breathing, (b) resonance, (c) vowel formation and attack, (d) the *sostenuto* (sustained tone), (e) the legato (slow scale, registers), (f) the *portamento,* (g) the *messa di voce,* (h) agility (coloratura, ornaments). Klein goes on to state, 'The old Italian teachers had no trouble in obtaining a bright, ringing tone. Resonance, therefore, may not have entered very largely into their theory, but was far from being ignored in their practice' (7).

Here, quite clearly, Klein mounts the bandwagon. The 'new bugaboo, Resonance' to which Herbert Witherspoon was to refer at a later time must, if one is 'with it,' be incorporated into the old scheme of things. Klein apparently had not realized that resonance is an event that occurs at the moment of tonal inception and is due to a precise positioning of the pharyngeal cavities. His was a typical state of mind which made the time ripe for the acceptance of Lilli Lehmann's propositions. Lehmann was one of the world's great singers and a strong advocate of learning through feeling (purely on an 'I feel it, therefore, you feel it' basis). If one is steeped in an older tradition and uncertain about the nature and cause of resonance, then it might be helpful to accept her idea that the sensations of vibrations felt in the palate, nose, and tongue are truly the cause of resonance. At the same time, DeReszke's postulate of nasal resonance (singing *dans la masque*) offered further inducement. But, if tone is to be resonated in the facial masque, it must be directed into and concentrated in that area. This led to techniques for volitionally 'placing' the tone to get it 'forward' into the frontal sinuses. There the vibrations could be concentrated and reinforced and the problem of resonance solved. No longer were teachers concerned with registration or a coordinative process which positioned the laryngeal and the oral pharynx. The new concepts of resonance would take care of everything.

How easy it is to part company with a functional truth. Nathan made a sharp distinction between tone and articulation, naming the nose, palate, teeth, and lips as auxiliaries. Garcia supported this view and observed that 'the real mouth of the singer ought to be considered the pharynx' (8). Dr. Marafioti, personal physician to Caruso and writer on vocal technique, chose to move toward the periphery and declared, 'Voice is speech, and is produced by the mouth and not by the vocal cords' (9).

Contemporary theorists have continued to move from the core to the periphery, following the path set by Lehmann and DeReszke. D. Ralph Appelman, in a book filled with harmonic analysis of tones and detailed description of the muscular processes involved in phonation, makes these comments on the subject of vowel formation:

> Each vowel represents certain well defined, physiological positions involving the tongue, labial orifice (lips), velum, mandible, and larynx, which have been determined by X-ray photographs and cinefluorography. TONGUE. To produce the basic vowel, the tip of the tongue must be placed against the bottom front teeth during phonation (production) of all vowel sounds sung on pitches within the area of stability. LIPS. In the high frontal, mid-frontal, and low frontal vowels, the lips are more spread than rounded. In the lowback, midback, and highback vowels, the lips are rounded progressively more than from lowback to highback positions. LARYNX. The laryngeal position is more lowered during phonation than the passive position assumed during normal breathing (10).

Another contemporary authority whose opinion carries considerable weight is William Vennard. He states, 'We are accustomed to think of the larynx as merely the vibrator, since it is the site of the vocal bands, but after all, it is a cavity. Startling as it may be, our most prized resonance may be here!' Later on, speaking of the ring in the voice, he observes, 'This ring has various characteristics that associate it with the larynx.' But this is getting too close to the functional core, because in a subsequent discussion of 'focus' and 'covering' he declares, 'The way to build a voice is from the front to the back, and not from the throat into the mouth. A means to this end is that synthetic consonant which I have called the "hum on the tongue." . . . This is an implement for achieving the correct "placement" of the tone, and thereby insuring its healthy development' (11).

In each of the above quotations, there is an all-pervasive theme: avoidance of a functional core for peripheral concerns. Appelman's 'well-defined, physiological positions' never arouse sufficient interest to develop a technique for influencing the positioning process at the point of tonal inception, for getting at the vocal organs and making them work from the inside. The idea of stimulating involuntary muscles is either abhorrent or never though of. All approaches seem to favor the plan advocated by Vennard and work to 'build a voice from front to back, and not from the throat into the mouth.'

This oversight is not peculiar to the scientifically oriented voice teacher. Almost all teachers in one form or another pursue an identical course. When the technique is 'throaty,' the suggested cure is to 'get the tone out of the throat' and to 'bring it forward,' obviously an avoidance of core activity. Tone is initiated in the throat, so the problem is not to get the tone 'out' of that area but to release the constricting tensions within it. The solution to this problem depends upon a program given over to *opening* the throat, in which the entire coordinative response of the organs involved in phonation is reversed.

If a stone is thrown into the water, the ripples will move out from the point of impact in a series of concentric circles. In this natural event, we have a perfect example of the meaning and purpose of functional vocal training. By developing techniques which energize the core of the vocal process, all peripheral matters will take care of themselves; the tongue will assume the correct position, there will be no jaw tension, the mouth and lips will position themselves normally, tones will not waver, there will be no wastage of breath, and quality will be individual, pure, and beautiful.

Now is the time for teachers to forget such irrelevancies as the Bernoulli effect, and pronouncements which state that 'in a position of rest the space between the wings of the thyroid is greatest, whereas in singing it may be a centimeter less,' and adopt principles based on natural order. Mancini had the right idea when he urged his scholars not to distrust 'the inclinations in regard to nature, which, when overlooked, make every attempt to overcome or correct by the aid of art, futile' (3).

There is a story told of a young Buddhist who went to a priest and said, 'Master, I want to be free.' The master replied, 'Who is binding you?' This story is pertinent because unless one is impatient with non-freedom, unless one wants to be free, functional training will fall on barren ground. Along with talent and other requisite gifts, the desire to fulfill one's potential is indispensable to the learning process. For those who have that desire, success, even in the face of adverse circumstances, can become a real possibility. The dream can become a reality.

Given this kind of desire and talent, the burden of instruction, especially in the beginning, falls upon the teacher. Many trees grow in the pine forest, but the tree that grows straightest, tallest, and most beautifully rounded is the one whose good fortune it has been to settle in the right environment. And environment is the teacher's direct responsibility. The exercises he selects, his understanding of functional mechanics, his sensitivity in knowing when to goad and when to coax, when to drive and when to relax, will determine whether or not the student's potential will be realized. Healthy life energy starts at the core and moves toward an outer periphery. Unless the work of 'unbinding' is core-directed, both physical and psychological potential will remain unfulfilled.

CHAPTER II

THE VOCAL MECHANISM

I F VOICE TRAINING techniques are to be reestablished on a practical basis, the first logical step would be to determine the kind of mechanism we are dealing with and the possible means at our disposal for improving its function. Superficially, we are concerned with the organs of voice, but a far more comprehensive view of the subject will be possible if the mechanism is recognized for what it truly is—a respiratory organ. Due to the fact that the respiratory system possesses those elements necessary for making tone, it can be readily converted into a sound-producing instrument. As such, it is being used as an adaptive mechanism. There are two phases to this process: 1) a series of muscular contractions which cause the vocal cords to adjust to the required length and tension for pitch, and 2) the positioning of the entire pharyngeal tract to answer the needs of resonance.

In rather simplistic terms, the vocal cords become vibratile by means of antagonistic tension having been brought to bear on the thyroarytenoid and the crico-thyroid and arytenoid muscles. The ratio of tension shared by each of these muscle groups determines registration. Concurrently, the laryngeal pharynx is moved into a position favorable to resonance by four muscles which hold it firmly suspended in the throat: the thyro-hyoid and stylo-pharyngeal muscles which raise the larynx, and the sterno-thyroid and crico-pharyngeal muscles which draw the larynx downward. When held in equilibrium, these enable the larynx to function as a primary resonator. Laryngeal resonance is, of course, also dependent upon the proper relaxation of the swallowing muscles. Thus, the act of phonation may be seen to be comprised of separate yet totally integrated activities.

'Voice,' therefore, is a product of function and has no mechanical function of its own. It is the end result of a coordinative process involving a complex of laryngeal and pharyngeal muscles, and all devices and techniques employed to improve the tone after the coordinative pattern has been set are useless. What a constructive program of vocal study *should* attempt is the discovery of a technique whereby the muscular coordination can be improved and perfected. As a correct vocal technique is rare, success in teaching and learning depends in large part upon a program given over to changing an habitual, i. e., faulty, coordinative process. The question is, how can the necessary changes be brought about?

The means available for employment as a stimulus control in singing are not hard to find. Because of the phenomenon of registration and its relationship to specific patterns of pitch and intensity, the vocal organs can be made to respond beyond the singer's power of volitional control, or, for that matter, even his preconcept. Consequently, new and predictable response patterns are easily induced, changing the way in which the air spaces surrounding the vocal cords are set into motion. When training techniques succeed in bringing the coordinative process into harmony with nature's laws, the end result, 'voice,' will show marked improvement. In the profoundest sense, this is the meaning of vocal training. It is the point of beginning where functional laws will reveal themselves to those who observe.

CHAPTER III

THE VOCAL REGISTERS

T HE FUNCTIONAL relationships within the organic structure of the vocal mechanism would fail to lend themselves to improvement were it not possible to isolate certain of the constituent parts. Fortunately, the whole mechanism is comprised of parts and, despite theoretical posturings, every singer and teacher of singing is familiar with the 'break' in the voice, the 'bridge,' and 'lifts,' as well as the various points of transition falling within the tonal range. Throughout the history of singing these isolated elements and subdivisions have been attributed to registration.

Several factors are influential in creating vocal segments. Principal among them are temperament, the size, shape and condition of the vocal organs, the combination and proportion of vocal faults, and the type of mechanical response made by the vocal organs as they adjust to meet changing conditions of pitch, intensity and the vowel. Chief among these factors is the natural correlation that exists between a particular pitch-intensity pattern and the physical adjustment assumed by the vocal cords. Unless this relationship is fully understood the task of restructuring a faulty coordinative process is all but impossible.

A register is a particular kind of physical adjustment assumed by the vocal organs in response to specific combinations of pitch and intensity.* The reason for this is plain: there is a direct correspondence between pitch, or frequency (the number of cycles traced by the vocal cords in one second), and the length, mass, and elasticity of the vibrating membrane. Intensity must also be considered a factor, insomuch as it is regulated by fluctuations of energy within the total system, as well as by the amplitude of the vocal cord movement.

Since the possible combinations of pitch, intensity, and the vowel are widely variable, corresponding changes must also take place in the length, mass and elasticity of the vocal folds. For such changes to be effective a delicate equilibrium must be established and maintained by the entire respiratory musculature. The significance of the term 'coordinative process' is that it indicates the *kind* of adjustment made by these muscles as they respond to the singer's mental concepts relating to pitch, intensity and the vowel.

Extreme differences in the length, mass and elasticity of the vocal cords create contrasting qualities called 'registers.' Particularly noteworthy is the fact that the physical adjustments are reflexive in nature, independent of preconcepts (unless through willful imposition), and inhibited solely by an imprecise muscular coordination. By recognizing the parallels that exist between pitch and intensity (registration), and a particular kind of muscular adjustment within the laryngeal pharynx, it is possible to take the mechanism apart, change the coordinative process, and reunite the total musculature in a more effective and useful way. In short, it becomes possible to restructure the vocal technique and recondition a badly conditioned reflex.

For the past century teachers of singing have, with rare exceptions, thought this procedure unwise, protesting what they call 'fragmenting' the voice. Any mechanism which works imperfectly,

---

*See: Appendix II: Historical Background of Registration.

however, if it is to be repaired properly, must be taken apart. The question, therefore, is not one of fragmentation, but one of functional mechanics. Clearly, if the mechanism is to be taken apart one must be skillful enough to put it back together again in better working order. Those who reject programs which 'fragment' the voice are those who, without exception, lack an understanding of functional mechanics.* If the voice were seamless, the entire concept of restructuring the technique, of changing an habitual coordinative process, of 'rebuilding' the voice, of making a dramatic technical improvement, would have to be abandoned.

Whether voices are seamless or fragmented, accounting must be made for the quality differences even the least discerning listener should be quick to recognize. As these differences are due to the structure and functioning of the vocal bands, it is necessary to examine the nature of those muscular tensions which are activated whenever the cords become vibratile.

REGISTRATION AND PITCH

THE MOVEMENT of the vocal cords is made possible by two important muscle groups to which they are attached, the crico-thyroids and the arytenoids. These groups interconnect with other parts of the respiratory system, their movement in normal respiration coinciding with each inspiratory and expiratory cycle. A primary function of the vocal cords, therefore, is to facilitate breathing, the glottis (the space between the vocal cords) alternately opening and closing to permit a free exchange of oxygen for carbon dioxide. One of the major objectives of correct vocalization runs counter to this natural tendency, as the cords must remain approximated rather than separated. For this

---

*Taking the voice apart should not be interpreted to mean 'dismantling' the mechanism. As a matter of fact, training procedures must be carried out in such a way as to leave the mechanism operable at all times. The awareness of things 'breaking down' stems more from psychological and conceptual disorientation than from an inability to make the vocal organs work as a harmonious unit.

reason special consideration must sometimes be given during training to breathing techniques (See BREATHING).

As the movement of these two muscular systems functioning
within the laryngeal pharynx is not subject to direct control, accessi-
bility becomes a real problem. How do they work? and what kind
of stimulus prompts them to move during phonation? Before sup-
plying an answer to the latter question we must first address ourselves to the former and further ask, what happens to the vocal
cords when a given pitch is sounded?

THE LOWER PITCH RANGE

IF WE CONSIDER first those tones belonging
to the lowest pitch range of the voice, it is obvious that the length
of the vibrating surface must be of optimum length and thickness,
thickness being more important than length. To accomplish this
the thyroarytenoids come into tension—they reflexively position
themselves in response to the singer's desire to sound a low pitch.
Since a muscle shortens when it contracts this has the effect of
increasing the mass of the vibrating surface. So arranged, the
cords are in an ideal 'set' for the articulation of lower pitch levels.

Throughout the process outlined above the crico-thyroids, natural antagonists to the arytenoids, offer but passive resistance to
the strong counter pull directed against them. In effect, their 'hold'
against the 'pull' of the arytenoids is slack. The increase in the
mass of the vibrating surface due to the dominance of arytenoid
tension introduces a homogeneous type of tonal texture commonly
recognized as the 'chest' register. Stringed instruments offer a
reasonable parallel to this physical arrangement as, in each case,
the thick strings are found in the lower tonal range, thinner stringing being reserved for the treble. Thickness and/or length also
influences the textural properties related to quality, quality *resulting* from the structural arrangements and physical adjustments
made in response to the demands of pitch, intensity and the vowel.

HIGHER PITCH LEVELS

I N ORDER to produce tones lying at higher pitch levels tension on the vocal cords must be increased. As there is a limit to the amount of tension that can be brought to bear when the cords are adjusted to their full length and thickness, their physical dimensions must of necessity be altered. In responding to this requirement the laryngeal muscles readjust, during which process the vocalis muscle (the internal thyroarytenoid) will relax somewhat, while simultaneously the crico-thyroids impose greater longitudinal tension on the vocal ligaments. Thus, the outer edges of the cords, through increased tension, become thinner and shorter. This process meets an essential requirement for the economical articulation of higher pitch levels: namely, a reduction in either the length or thickness of the vibrating surface.

Should an increase in crico-thyroid tension be accompanied by an insufficient 'holding' action on the part of the thyroarytenoids, the vocal cords will be able to offer much less resistance to the breath pressure than would otherwise be the case. Because of the absence of essential arytenoid tension the antagonistic muscular contractions which maintain the natural equilibrium of the vocal instrument are destroyed. Under these circumstances the glottal space will remain open, permitting the breath to escape unchecked. This immediately transforms the tonal characteristics previously in effect, the 'chesty' quality disappears, and the resonance becomes devitalized. Now the voice is bodiless and 'hooty.' An isolated registration of this kind produces a homogeneous tone quality commonly referred to as 'falsetto,' a register notable for its breathiness.

The homogeneous sounds recognized as the 'chest' and falsetto registers may now be seen to be the product of a particular kind of muscular adjustment within the laryngeal pharynx. This knowledge affords an important insight into the voice-building process because, while the laryngeal musculature cannot be volitionally positioned, nevertheless that position can be influenced through the mechanics of registration. One of the most important aspects of that influence is pitch, the mental concept to which the vocal organs respond. But pitches can be sung either loudly or softly, and pitch of itself is not the determining factor in registration. Pitch coupled with intensity, however, is.

REGISTRATION AND INTENSITY

To AN EXTENT far greater than commonly believed, the contour and physical adjustment of the vocal folds have a direct bearing upon intensity. In lower pitch ranges the thickness of the cords reduces the size of the glottal space. Consequently, the cords are maintained in a parallel position for a longer period of time than would otherwise be the case. In this process normal respiration is arrested, resulting in a buildup of air pressure which is then periodically released in a series of 'puffs.' Because compression has been built up within each puff of air there is, as a result, a sharp rise in intensity.

With the cords adjusted to their full length and thickness the amplitude of vibration caused by the puffs is also correspondingly greater. Because of this amplitude the glottal space will open rather widely with each wavelike movement of the cords. The result is an intensity increase directly proportionate to the increase of amplitude. Additionally, much of the harmonic richness imparted to a tone derives from this same amplitude. As these movements are extremely complex, frequencies are sounded other than the fundamental, the effect of which is to enrich the tone harmonically as well as increase its intensity.*

---

*Authorities are divided as to the cause of this wavelike motion. There are those who believe that suction, produced by the fact that air in motion has less density or pressure than air that is not in motion (the Bernoulli effect), causes pitch changes which are due to reduced lateral pressure on the vocal folds and not directly related to the lengthening, thinning, tightening or loosening of the vocal cords themselves. The more conventional view is that pitch is dependent upon tension in the vocal bands brought on by a complicated interplay within the total musculature of the respiratory system. Those who believe in the air pressure theory seem, in the writer's view, to have put the cart before the horse.

Homogeneous sounds recognizable as the chest register, therefore, are not only associated with the lowest portion of the tonal range, but with higher levels of intensity as well.

THE 'BREAK'

As a VIBRATOR of a given length and thickness cannot tolerate excessive tension and responds by breaking so, too, the voice will break off and crack when the chest register, a product of the physical adjustment described, is forced too high. When such a break occurs the distinctive tone quality which suddenly appears is that homogeneous quality recognized as a falsetto.

The physical arrangement which takes place after a register 'break' has occurred represents a dramatic shift from one type of coordinative process to another. Now, instead of maintaining their former position of approximation, the vocal cords will separate somewhat and acquire sharp, tautened edges. This decreases the amplitude of movement (the normal, pleasant vibrations which introduce a 'singy' quality to the voice), sharply reduces the intensity, and permits excessive amounts of breath to escape unchecked. Because of the absence of almost all vibratory impulse due to deficient amplitude the tones emitted become 'straight,' breathy, comparatively weak, and lacking in harmonic richness; in short, false.

Tone is, obviously, the product of complex sound waves emitted as a result of pressure variations created by escaping puffs of air. But were it not for the fact that this pressure is built up by a proper positioning of the vocal folds themselves, such a pressure system would be inefficient and yield poor tone quality. It is far more likely that the wavelike motion is caused by a healthy coordinative process which finds the thyro-vocalis and the aryvocalis muscles, which divide the vocal cords into two equal segments, together with the thyroarytenoids, weaving a complex pattern whose movement contour creates a constantly varying series of harmonics within the fundamental.

THE FALSETTO

T̂HE FALSETTO in its pure form is confined within a range of approximately one octave. This holds true for all voice types, both male and female. It is a difficult mechanism to understand. There are many false tones which are obviously falsetto *derived,* yet not a pure falsetto. What features, then, distinguish the pure falsetto from those tones which are falsetto derived?

When reference is made to the pure falsetto, or isolated upper register, the tones must possess the following identifiable features: 1) a range limited to, at most, an octave for all voice types, male and female, 2) an extremely 'breathy' and 'hooty' tone quality, 3) a high rate of breath expulsion which restricts tonal duration to but three or four seconds at best, 4) little or no aesthetic value, 5) a total absence of tonal pulse, and 6) an inability to swell or diminish on any single tone without reflexively engaging some chest register tension. When tones become clear and the range extensive, when tones can be swelled and diminished, when there is a natural vibrancy, or when the mechanism becomes flexible, then the falsetto can no longer be said to be pure.

Judged by this standard, a singer who might be described as capable of 'singing and sustaining beautiful falsetto tones' would not be using a pure falsetto. On the basis of the above measurement it is obvious that a 'sustained, beautiful falsetto' is a falsetto derived tone, a coordinated falsetto—one in which, to a degree, the chest register acts as a participating agent.* Tonal clarity,

---

*Here we touch upon one of the major stumbling blocks to effective scientific research on voice. Some trained singers exhibit one set of characteristics, other trained singers another. Untrained singers likewise yield contrary characteristics. The fact is, all research must contain some element of error until such time as a number of perfectly used voices can be tested and evaluated. As no such voices now exist, or have ever existed, there is little hope for a completely satisfactory resolution to this and other technical problems related to voice. The 'average' singer sings badly, and healthy functional norms cannot be established by accumulating data based upon the performance of the average singer.

the ability to sustain tone, the presence of a musical quality, and other normally desirable features cannot exist without some measure of coordinate action with the thyroarytenoids (the chest register). A purse falsetto is without chest register connection, does not sustain, and is far from beautiful.

A raw chest register and the 'hooty' pure falsetto are the basic mechanisms which Garcia and others described as homogeneous sounds and are tone qualities yielded by a particular type of physical arrangement within the laryngeal musculature. By understanding how the registers work while in their more primitive form, one is led to a fuller understanding of the functional properties of the mechanism as it operates at more sophisticated levels of vocalization. Simply by understanding the pitch-intensity patterns which evoke a predictable response, important changes can be made in the behavior of those laryngeal muscles which normally lie beyond the power of volitional control.

When the register mechanisms operate as relatively isolated entities, the voice is incapable of functioning as a singing instrument. The range of each register when separated is too short and lacking in quality to serve an aesthetic purpose, nor can effective sound be made in the area of the register transition. What is important, however, is the insight provided by several discoveries: 1) that 'voice' is the product of vibrations set in motion by the vocal cords, vibrations whose efficiency is determined by the kind of muscular adjustment made within the laryngeal musculature, 2) that these adjustments are made possible by a delicate interplay between two muscle groups and their auxiliaries, the crico-thyroids and the arytenoids, and 3) that the important functional activities involved in phonation are non-volitional and occur reflexively as a response to specific patterns of pitch and intensity.

The dynamics of registration may now be seen to provide the teacher of voice with the necessary tools for getting at laryngeal muscles whose activity lies beyond the power of volitional control. In correcting vocal errors, therefore, the kind of instruction which encourages the student to *act upon* his vocal organs (such as 'placing' the voice, 'bringing the tone forward,' adding nasal resonance, preparing mouth and tongue positions, and controlling the breath) is either useless or superficial. A more correct procedure would be to concentrate exclusively on the pitch-intensity pattern projected (the influence of the vowel on registration will be discussed later) and naturalness of posture. If the scale pattern has been wisely selected it, of itself, will cause the involuntary musculature of the larynx to respond more favorably. Movements prompted by this type of stimulus will be natural and have the advantage of transcending the dictates of the singer's will, his conditioned reflexes, and even his preconcepts as they relate to aesthetic goals.*

REGISTER COORDINATION

A COMBINED REGISTRATION finds the vocal organs readjusting in somewhat the following manner: each rise in pitch is met by a corresponding increase of tension on the lateral crico-arytenoid, the posterior arytenoid, and the crico-thyroid muscles, as well as the inner fibres of the vocalis muscles. Because of their attachment to the thyroid cartilage the crico-thyroids also cause the upper part of the voice box (the Adam's apple) to tilt forward slightly. The combined action of these elements influences the physical adjustment of the vocal cords making them longer, thinner and capable of assuming greater tension.

With the vocal cords adjusted in the fashion described a different kind of tone quality emerges, a quality variously referred to as the middle voice, the middle register, or the middle range. A more practical way of viewing the matter, however, is to recognize the quality of the tones straddling the 'break' as being a representation of the textural properties contributed by the two mechanisms, the chest register and the falsetto, which have now been joined.

---

*See: Appendix III, Functional Studies, for procedures which will reveal the mechanics of registration.

When the cords are able to vibrate freely at their full length, even though the inner folds have relaxed and the outer edges are thinner, there is a point at which this adjustment, too, will have outlived its usefulness, higher frequencies requiring a further change in the contour of the vibrating surface. To meet this exigency the cords assume yet another adjustment, one having an effect similar to the fingering used in the playing of the violin, where the vibrating portion of the string is shortened by 'stopping.' In singing, the shortening of the vibrating surface is brought about by the gradual adduction of the vocal cords.

ADDUCTION

THE ADDUCTION of the vocal folds is a process which finds the posterior portion of the cord meeting and pressing together, thus shortening the anterior segment which has been left free to vibrate. An exact parallel to this process is the common zipper which, when made to close, gradually reduces the aperture above the adducted parts. During phonation, as greater portions of the vocal folds adduct and make contact, the glottal space becomes smaller and the vibrating surface of the cords thinner. This leaves the mechanism in an ideal 'set' for the phonation of pitches lying in higher tonal areas.

The adduction of the vocal cords begins, in terms of aural recognition, at the point of the register 'break.' At the precise moment the posterior portion of the thyroarytenoid comes together and approximates, a new balance, or ratio of tension, is established between the participating mechanisms. This change of registration takes place in all voice types, male and female, at roughly the same pitch, namely, E above middle C.

The adduction of the vocal folds finds the mechanism operating effectively as a unit. With the muscular contractions so adjusted it may be seen how each tone in the musical scale has its own ratio of registration. Given the fact that the balance is precise, the muscles developed to a high state of tonicity, and the larynx well-positioned, the vocal technique now may be said to be ideal. When the coordinative process is so arranged the pedagogic aim would be to establish concepts related to function which would preserve intact a technique which is already correct. Few voices, however, belong in this category. A faulty coordinative process is far more common, with the vocal teacher's concern centering almost exclusively on correction rather than preservation.

Movements characteristic of the vocal cords as they phonate and participate in the respiratory process are shown in Figure 1. Obviously, the adjustments depicted involve a process which represents the physical substance of the singer's technique. Through the dynamics of registration the laryngeal muscles, although involuntary, can be made to readjust and coordinate more efficiently in the phonative process by means of the procedures here advocated.

FIGURE I

courtesy of Brodnitz

Fig. I. Showing three examples out of the almost infinite variety of adjustments the vocal cords are capable of making. It is obvious that each different position of the cords requires an intricate readjustment on the part of the participating laryngeal musculature. Obviously, the positioning processes are made in response to the four basic components present in every tone—pitch, intensity, vowel and duration. The pictures shown have been taken from Bell Telephone photographs appearing in *Keep Your Voice Healthy* by Frederic S. Brodnitz.

CHAPTER IV

REGISTER DEVELOPMENT

IN RATHER rudimentary fashion the preceding discussion has attempted to establish a direct correspondence between a given pitch-intensity pattern and the muscular adjustments assumed by the organs of voice. But, although the thyroarytenoid muscle *can,* for example, when properly adjusted, relax and shorten the vocal ligament, approximate the vocal folds, pull them apart by their lateral contraction, aid in raising and lowering the pitch, vary the length and thickness of the vibrating segment, and tense one portion of the vocal folds while the remainder relaxes, it and its auxiliary musculature can also *fail* to do so effectively. Therefore, while the vocal mechanism may ideally be considered a functional unit, the unitary relationship is usually faulty and must be changed. At this level, training procedures must establish the 'break' in the voice, develop and recoordinate the constituent parts, and in general reverse those procedures previously in effect.

Unless the technique is well-formed, vocal training should

commence with the disengagement of a wrongly adjusted registration. To understand this process a hypothetical condition of
absolute 'purity' must be postulated. Such an isolated, or 'pure'
registration is shown in Figure II.

FIGURE II

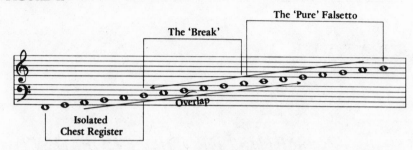

FIG. II. Indicating the boundaries of the 'pure' falsetto and the isolated
chest register. This is obviously a primitive non-singing arrangement, but
it does reveal the inner dynamics of the vocal process. Once a coordinate
relationship between the two basic mechanisms has been established
the range extends remarkably, while at the same time the tonal properties normally associated with singing gradually appear. How these two
elemental divisions lead logically to numerous subdivisions is shown in
Fig. V. Of particular interest is the position of the 'break' which, as
the registers coordinate, increasingly narrows as the inner portions of
each mechanism move toward the other (see arrows). Thus the 'break'
is ultimately confined to a semi-tone or two at E, above middle C, with
women's voices, and F, with higher men's voices.

Thoughtful analysis of Figure II will reveal several interesting
facts: 1) one register is located in the upper range of the voice,
the other, in the lower, 2) the range of each is extremely short
and, therefore, without functional utility, 3) the upper portion
of the chest register and the lower portion of the falsetto are at
opposite extremes with regard to intensity, 4) both male and
female voices are hypothetically capable of singing a 'pure' falsetto, and 5) in a literal sense an absolutely 'pure' registration as
here defined is non-functional.

In addition to the observations listed above other conclusions
may be drawn. From comments made earlier with reference to
the textural properties associated with registration it is clear that

a serious disparity exists between the two isolated mechanisms as to resonance characteristics, texture and quality. Also, due to the high degree of breath expulsion native to the falsetto and the excessive force needed to activate the pure chest register, sustained vocalization under this arrangement is impossible. On the positive side, however, when, as in a 'mixed' (an improperly combined) registration, it is necessary to recoordinate the muscular responses, Figure II. does indicate the context within which the exercise selected must be contained in restoring the mechanisms to their rightful place.

There are but three factors to be considered when attempting to divide the registration: 1) the proper pitch on which to commence, 2) the correct level of intensity, and 3) the selection of an appropriate vowel. More will be said about vowels shortly, but the 'ah' vowel is an essential aid in establishing the chest register, the 'oo' when working with the falsetto. It is also important to bear in mind that a narrow gap between the mechanisms is most practical, a slight separation being sufficient to permit independent development and realignment. Total elimination of the 'break' is an error to be avoided, as no fundamental improvement of the registration is possible once the parts are completely unified.

The procedure to be followed in disengaging a wrongly combined registration, then, would seem to be as follows. First, the weaker or non-existent register must be established. With women's voices this will usually be the chest register; with men's voices, the falsetto. Because of the restricted tonal area to which each isolated register is confined the most practical exercise will be limited to a single tone. At the outset it is also advisable to select a pitch lying somewhere in the middle of each register: B, below middle C, being a proper starting point for the female chest register; E, above middle C, being appropriate for the male falsetto. The second step is to exercise each register, within the confines of its pitch range, until each mechanism is capable of participating in the coordinative process.

A 'pure' registration as here described is incompatible with functional singing. Such a technique finds the voice without quality, range, flexibility, resonance or freedom. What this discussion should indicate, however, is the outline of the tonal boundaries within which each register operates when completely isolated, as well as the need for combining them. A truly 'pure' registration should never be encouraged except in the rarest instances.

THE REGISTER OVERLAP

NEW PROCEDURES must be introduced to unify the registers and of immediate interest is the tendency of the two mechanisms to overlap as they move toward one another and share several pitches in common. Of the four tones so shared (B below middle C, to the E above) those belonging to the falsetto are weak in intensity, breathy in quality and have little duration potential. The chest register possesses opposite characteristics, being of high intensity (rather rough and non-aesthetic), yet capable of being sustained without undue loss of breath. A program given over to voice 'building' must take these factors into account, reconcile the differences, unify the parts, and at the same time remove those constrictor tensions which interfere with an open-throated resonance adjustment.

Since the registers appear reflexively in response to intensity, balancing them in the vicinity of the 'break' is achieved by regulating the intensity. In much the same manner that weights are balanced on a scale, each overlapped part must be adjusted until a perfect equilibrium is attained. A normal procedure would be to strengthen the weaker mechanism while holding the development of the other in abeyance, a practice which must be continued until such time as the registers have been made to match in quality and development.

Inasmuch as the chest register should not be moved higher than E above middle C, efforts to extend the range and narrow the gap in the 'break' area must center on the development of the falsetto.

Whether the voice be high or low, male or female, it is the falsetto which must be transformed into a legitimate tone quality and made to become the dominant element in the singer's technique. This is not to suggest that the chest register is to be neglected, or even considered subordinate; for unless each mechanism is made to participate as a co-equal partner the voice will never mature properly. A point worth remembering is this: singing in the full voice is impossible without a well-developed and integrated chest register, while soft singing is impossible without a coordinated falsetto. Furthermore, a correctly sung forte is a legitimate extension of a properly sung pianissimo, neither extreme of loudness being correct unless the falsetto has been effectively integrated into the technique.*

Due to the physical peculiarities of each register the choice of scale patterns suitable for uniting the mechanisms is rather limited. Nevertheless, several practical courses seem obvious: 1) one which takes advantage of the relative weakness of the lowest tones of the chest register, building an ascending arpeggio on those pitches, 2) a procedure which seeks to maintain an even level of intensity throughout the entire compass of the chest register *despite each rise in pitch,* and 3) one in which the intensity level of the falsetto is diminished coincident with the outward extension of the range, which should now be encouraged to overlap the entire chest register. In the latter instance, this procedure should reflexively coordinate the falsetto with the chest register, introduce greater tonal clarity to both mechanisms, reduce the amount of energy expended, and eliminate tonal breathiness.

The first two procedures suggested above merit further comment. Concurrent with the development of the registers in the manner described the factor of open-throated resonance must be taken into account. As it is the chest register which acts as the

---

*To those who may be overzealous in joining the registers and attempt to do so prematurely, it must be stressed that certain prerequisites have to be met before it is advisable to seal the registration. There must be relatively little constrictor tension present and each of the two mechanisms must be at full strength before being fully integrated. What has not been developed before the registers have been joined can never be developed after they have been combined.

throat opening agent (the falsetto being more intimately associated with the muscular system used in swallowing i. e., natural
constrictors—see THE ATTACK), this mechanism must be effectively engaged at all times. Unless the falsetto is linked to the
chest register in such a way as to ensure an open-throated resonance adjustment the entire purpose of joining the two will have
been aborted, as failure to unite them properly will make the tone
either tremulous or wobbly. To avert throat constriction, therefore, exercises must be constructed which will establish the chest
register with sufficient strength so as to cause the throat to open,
but not so strongly as to push out the desired participation of the
falsetto.

Another consideration when uniting the registers is the singer's
sex. As women sing an octave higher than men their chest register will be short-ranged, whereas with men the shorter ranged
mechanism will be the falsetto. Such differences, while superficial,
will nevertheless dictate the character of the scale patterns selected
when developing the registration and will, indeed, represent differences which are more apparent than real. The sole difference
among any of the voice types, male or female, is the natural range
of the voice with respect to the register 'break.'

The most practical scale to be employed in developing and in-
tegrating the falsetto with the chest register is a full octave arpeggio. Initially, it was stated that a reduction in the intensity level
of the pure falsetto would eliminate its breathy and 'hooty' quality.
While this is true, nevertheless one must guard against the intrusion of constrictor tensions. Should the voice shut off, the clear
falsetto must be abandoned and another approach taken. As it
is desirable to establish a head register dominated technique, work
on the falsetto must continue, but in its pure form. The fact that
the pure falsetto is being made to expand over a wide pitch range
will, of course, introduce some measure of chest register coordination. The danger of following this procedure is that the registers
will 'mix,' and avoidance of this pitfall largely depends upon the
teacher's skill and acuity of hearing.

Every effort should now be made to extend the falsetto mechanism outwardly in both directions over as wide a pitch range as seems feasible. Consequently, it is essential that the musical figure be lengthened, first, by adding a third, then a fifth and, finally, by including the double octave. This procedure should maintain the desirable open-throatedness, help the registers to draw together, merge their characteristics, and rebalance them of their own volition.

At the outset the tonal texture of the extended falsetto indeed sounds 'false,' but this condition will soon rectify itself. Correct practice will reflexively coordinate the two mechanisms and introduce greater tonal clarity, with the falsetto finally developing into what is commonly recognized as the 'head' voice. Subsequent development should proceed in much the same manner one builds a seven layer cake—layer upon layer of intensity being added until the full voice appears. This is the underlying technique for executing the messa di voce (the art of swelling and diminishing the tone), that most beautiful artistic effect so rarely heard. A technique so constructed, incidentally, will never permit the singer to fall into the error of singing softly one way and loudly another.

The most suitable vowels for developing and extending the range of the falsetto in the manner suggested are 'oo,' 'ee,' and 'ah.' Of the three, it is preferable to commence with the 'ah,' as an open vowel tends to add more chest register to the falsetto than would otherwise be the case.

With the emergence of a clear falsetto (now a coordinated falsetto, or 'head' voice), attention must be given to restructuring the chest register. To make this register aesthetically acceptable the rough quality natural to it when isolated must undergo a change. The most practical approach is to build an arpeggio on a low G (applicable for both male and female voices in their respective voice ranges, although the tenor and soprano could commence a step higher if necessary), using the vowel 'ah,' at an intensity level which represents an equitable balance between the two register mechanisms. The purpose of this exercise, of course, is to engage both registers from the start and maintain their unitary relationship.

Again, it must be stressed that when one practices this exercise, neither the intensity nor the energy level should increase as the pitch rises. Another error to be avoided is to 'cover,' or 'hook,' into the higher tones in the area of the register transition. A perfect legato must be maintained and the vowel kept pure; otherwise both the registration and the resonance adjustment will be imprecise.

Several advantages will have been gained by observing the foregoing: 1) the slightly lowered intensity of the upper tones will reflexively hold back the aggressive tendency of the chest register, thus inviting greater falsetto participation, 2) the resonance will be vitalized, 3) the quality will become more musical, and 4) the gap in the 'break' area will be narrowed. Equally important, by having started with a balanced registration on the lowest tones of the arpeggio the sturdy qualities of the chest register will fill out the voice, ensure an open-throated resonance adjustment, promote durability, and develop a technique suitable for full-voiced singing. Additional possibilities for growth are to be found in the continued exploitation of the falsetto which, in its coordinated form, must ultimately become the dominant element in the singer's technique.

The balancing process here outlined must be continued until such time as the two register mechanisms are perfectly blended and able to perform as a functional unit. Just blending them, however, is not sufficient; they must be combined in such a way as to achieve the fullest possible range extension (normally running two and one-half octaves with men to three with women), while at the same time enhancing the resonance characteristics and overall flexibility.

SYNERGY VS. ENERGY

I T SHOULD NOW be apparent that two separate and distinct types of procedure have been outlined: one applicable to a process given over to separating and developing the registers as independent elements, the other, to procedures designed to unite them. The physiological difference between these requires a distinction to be made between synergy and energy.

When accounting was made for a rise in pitch it was remarked that this could be accomplished in three ways: 1) by utilizing the chest register, thus forcing the intensity to increase with the rise in pitch, 2) by breaking off at a certain point into the falsetto, and 3) by establishing the coordinated falsetto, or head voice (brought about by employing variations of the messa di voce) which merges the two mechanisms into a functional unit. In the first instance the rise in intensity brought about a corresponding increase in arytenoid tension, an increase which ultimately caused the voice to 'break.' Over and against this, the pure falsetto, after the 'break' had occurred, was the result of tension having been transferred to the crico-thyroids. To avoid throat constriction each of these isolated elements had to be used energetically.

The third arrangement, the coordinated falsetto, or head voice, results from an entirely different process. With both mechanisms working together simultaneously, each rise in pitch is met by increased tension on the crico-thyroids, while at the same time the arytenoids hold against their pulling action. This distinction is important to an understanding of a combined registration and involves a concept having to do with synergy and energy.

A synergic activity is one in which a muscle, or a muscle group, holds against the contraction of another group against which it acts as a natural antagonist. Thus, when a contracting muscle is energized it may be said to be dynamically active, whereas the stabilizing muscle group will synergetically hold against the pull. This distinction is a key factor in understanding the relationship between a coordinated registration and one which finds the registers either isolated, imbalanced, or incorrectly energized. A correct technique finds the chest register working synergetically and holding against the pull of the energized head voice.*

---

*With these considerations in mind, it may be seen that efforts to restructure the technique will often move in contrary directions. In terms of correct singing those procedures given over to separating the registers are going the

The concept of a register response as an aggressive action in one tonal area and a passively active response in another is one of the keys to understanding the singing voice. In the pitch range from C, above middle C, to the upper reaches of the voice range the 'head' register is dynamic and participates actively. In the tonal area below the 'break,' however, this mechanism, though still active, must yield to the stronger contraction of the chest register. To a certain extent, the aggressive chest register poses a serious pedagogic problem, and care must be taken in the tonal range extending from E flat, below middle C, to the octave above, that this mechanism is not permitted to push the head register out of action and cause the two to separate.

The theory of the reacting pattern of the registers as a 'hold against a pull' clarifies many facets of technique. It accounts for the rotary action of the registers (see: REGISTER ROTATION) as well as explaining the difference between vigorous, dramatic singing and 'pushing.' A correctly energized and synergized registration contributes importantly to the total equilibrium of the vocal function and marks the point at which the singer is ready to seriously come to grips with tone 'color' as it relates to interpretation. For all of the seeming complexity of this concept in terms of practical application, however, both energic and synergic activities can be induced through the mechanics of registration and its natural correlatives—pitch, intensity, and the vowel.

RATIOS OF REGISTRATION

I N a correctly combined registration both mechanisms must be engaged regardless of the pitch and intensity being

---

wrong way. However, in terms of restructuring the coordinative process and rebuilding the voice, they are absolutely essential. How to restructure the technique, yet at the same time keep the voice functionally operative, is the tightrope every teacher directly concerned with improving the interior function of the laryngeal musculature must walk if his work is to be effective.

sung. The essential difference is one of proportion, in the ratio of tension shared between them. How this tension is distributed, and the probable manner in which the muscles participate, are more than an interesting speculation. A theoretical understanding should lead to more effective technical training and give meaning to the scales and exercises employed in developing the voice.

Garcia's classic definition of a register describes the two mechanisms as being a series of homogeneous sounds, each having its own area of tonal effectiveness. Further, each group of contrasting qualities, i. e., homogeneous sounds, was thought to be due to a separate type of mechanical arrangement within the vocal organs. Each set of contrasting qualities was then equated with changes in the length and thickness of the vocal cords brought on by corresponding differences in the contraction of those laryngeal muscles holding them in position. An additional parallel was discovered to exist between these events and the response of the vocal organs to pitch and intensity, a response which determined the type of registration in effect.

A properly developed registration is one in which the activity of each register is properly combined with the other. In moving over a wide range of pitch and intensity, therefore, it is essential that an equitable ratio of tension be distributed between the two mechanisms and maintained at all times. Ideally, there is a different ratio of tension for each pitch, intensity and vowel pattern being sung—in effect, diversity within unity. Few singers are sufficiently well-advanced, however, to meet this standard, and a slight 'break' is not only common, but in most instances desirable.

While it is often permissible to have a 'break' between the registers the gap must never be so wide as to prohibit complete freedom of access and egress. Certainly the discrepancy should not be so great, except for special interpretive effects, as to create the impression that the singer is using two separate voices. To habitually change from one register to the other will erode the technique and separate rather than join the registers. A concept far more useful is to consider the shifting ratios in terms of addition and subtraction.

Needless to say, the vocal mechanism will yield far better results when working as a unit than it will when either register is operating on its own. The question is: if the proportion of tension shared by each register increases and decreases with fluctuating patterns of pitch and intensity, how is this proportion to be determined?

A definitive answer to this question is provided by the exercise known as the messa di voce. Traditionally, the art of the messa di voce (or swelled tone) requires a gradual crescendo from pianissimo to the full voice. Since the chest register indentifies with forte levels of intensity, this mechanism could hardly be expected to play a prominent role in executing such a figure. A more correct execution would be to commence in the coordinated 'head' register, whose intrinsic nature is soft both as to dynamics and texture, and gradually increase the intensity until its strength potential has been exhausted. As the coordinated 'head' voice quality contains some degree of chest register participation, both mechanisms will be simultaneously engaged, but with the burden of effort being assumed by the upper register. Under such an arrangement the chest register will synergetically 'hold' against the increased pull of the 'head' voice, vitalizing the softest tones, thus cementing the coordinate relationship between the participating elements. In a technique so structured the 'holding' action of the chest register will always be directly proportionate to the 'pulling' strength of the 'head' voice.

From the standpoint of ease and facility, this arrangement offers many advantages. The singer does not have to release one register before engaging the other, so the necessary transitions can be made gracefully. Another benefit is an absence of muscular interference, a fact which should further enhance the singer's sense of ease and freedom. Additionally, the technical situation contains within itself the means for gradually swelling and diminishing from one intensity to another, one vowel to another, and one pitch range to another without awkward shifts and changes. The singer who has properly coordinated his registration (provided there is an absence of throat constriction) is vocally free.

REGISTER SEGMENTS

W ITH the registers functioning as a unit one is struck by the fact that, apart from the area of the register 'break,' there are other noticeable points of transition that merit comment. These are the 'lifts,' or segments, which appear to divide the singer's tonal range into special categories.

Despite certain similarities between a segmenting action and a break in the registration there are fundamental differences. A register is determined by a particular type of mechanical activity in which one muscle group dominates the other, the 'break' representing a dramatic shift in tension from one group to its natural antagonist. Opposed to this, a segmenting action will occur when the two mechanisms work together as a coordinate unit. While varying somewhat according to the weight of the voice, the 'lifts,' or segments, are observable on identical pitches (provided the voice is reasonably well used) regardless of the singer's sex or voice type. They are shown in Figure III.

Significantly, it is the outline of both the pure and the coordinated falsetto which coincides with the points at which segments are recognizable. As previously stated, the range of the pure falsetto extends from B below middle C to the octave above. Success in introducing some degree of coordinate action, however, will extend its boundaries outwardly in both directions. Thus, the segmenting points closest to the register 'break' are identifiable with the pitches at which the pure falsetto terminates, whereas the segmental pitches on the far side of the 'break,' F below middle C, and the F lying an octave and a fourth above, mark the outer boundaries of the coordinated falsetto.* Physically, the transition tones which outline the various segments are caused by subtle changes in the length and thickness of the vibrating sur-

---

*If one chooses to make a distinction between the coordinated falsetto and the head voice it can be made on this basis: the 'head' voice develops beyond the boundaries set by the coordinated falsetto and becomes qualitatively different.

FIGURE III

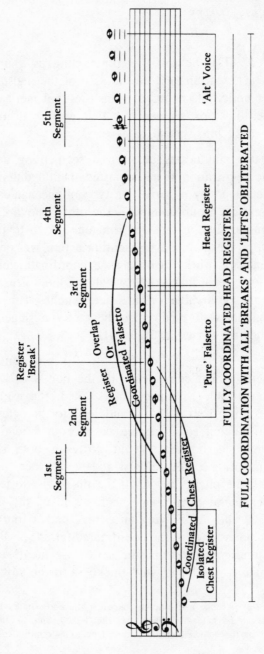

Fɪɢ. III. Showing the five segmental points as they evolve out of a coordinate relationship between the two basic mechanisms—the chest register and the falsetto. Those who possess well-formed voices (having at least two to three octaves tonal range) will have little difficulty in recognizing the textures and the transition points which define the boundaries recorded above.

face of the vocal cords as they readjust to meet individual pitch requirements.

The range of the coordinated falsetto roughly approximates the middle tonal range of many voice types and is often considered to be the product of a third register mechanism. No justification exists for such a belief, however, since there is no mechanism to account for such a phenomenon. A coordinated falsetto is just that, a falsetto which has achieved effective contact with the chest register mechanism. True, there is a distinct 'color' difference because of this connection, but this does not necessarily mean that a third mechanism is operative, any more than one can say that green is a primary color because of its uniqueness. Furthermore, one must ask, 'the middle of what?' Is the middle of the short ranged voice identical to the middle of one that is long ranged? This does not seem to be so. Is the middle range of the coloratura the same as that of the mezzo-soprano? Obviously not. Concepts such as a middle register must be discarded as useless and misleading. There is no way a voice can be properly trained when a nonexistent 'mechanism' is treated as though it operated on a mechanical principle.

In acknowledging the various segmental areas falling within the tonal range it is also important to recognize that these interadjustments must take place within the framework of an unchanging resonance adjusment. A constant resonance adjustment is basic to correct singing and must be maintained despite the changing ratios of registration. My own inclination is to quarrel with the word 'lift' to describe the transition points, as the very act of 'lifting' logically leads to the 'up and over' concept so commonly urged on students to their detriment. Rather than 'up and over' and 'lifting' there must be a continuous feeling of overall connection from below, with the tonal flow moving uninterruptedly from the lowest to the uppermost tones of the voice on a perfect legato.

Another point worth remembering is that the higher intensities formerly desirable when the registers were relatively isolated are no longer applicable. Now the tonal area lying between C and F (curiously, the upper C to F area in both the male and the female

voice although for the respective voices each lies an octave apart)
requires a *reduction* in volume, rather than an increase. If the
chest register is to 'hold against the pull' of the head voice, the
singer must be encouraged to hold back both the intensity and
the amount of energy expended. This practice will permit the
head register to become the dominant singing mechanism and
avoid 'pushing' because of an overly dominant chest register.

TEXTURE, REGISTRATION AND
SENSATIONS OF VIBRATION

WHETHER OR NOT the 'seams' in the voice
are detectable, the textural properties of the coordinated falsetto,
or head voice, and the chest register will always be discernible to
the functionally aware listener. Such influences, of course, are
more easily recognizable at wider extremes of range and intensity
than they are on middle ground. High tones at low levels of
intensity are obviously dominated by a texture growing out of the
head register; low tones at high levels of intensity by the chest
register. The middle tonal range at intermediate intensity, however, being comprised of roughly equal proportions of each register, makes both the vocal segments and the textural properties
associated with registration qualitatively more obscure.

In view of the fact that each register awakens strong sensations
of vibration seemingly located in the 'chest' and in the 'head,' an
awareness of these sensations can also be used to reinforce the
total impression received from textural sources. Thus, the singer
should be able to identify with the functional activities at work
within his instrument in several ways: 1) he can recognize the
specific area in which the sensations of vibration are centered, 2)
he can learn to equate the special textural properties of tone quality
detectable within the various segmental areas with a particular
kind of register balance (which, like pitch, is also responsive to
concepts), and 3) he can knowingly utilize specific combinations

of pitch, intensity and the vowel which will yield both the desirable textural properties and the sensations of vibrations which accompany them. In addition, he will be very much aware of the 'rolling,' or 'rotating' action of the registers as the voice moves from a position of 'lower' resonance to one of 'higher' resonance. These sensations, while an acoustic illusion, are nevertheless a vital part of the singer's sensual awareness.

Movement from one tonal area to another, then, is always accompanied by modifications of tonal texture. Although these modifications are related to corresponding changes in the positioning of the vocal organs, nevertheless the singer can both *hear* and *feel* the changes taking place. It is the singer's awareness of movement, the going from one balance of blended registration to another, that gives rise to the impression of there being a rotary action of the registers. Since the sensations of vibration associated with the 'head' register appear to be higher in position and those of the 'chest' register lower, the awareness of movement to and from each area is very real.

Physiologically, however, it is the contraction of the cricothyroid and arytenoid muscle groups which causes the apparent rotary action of the registers. The cords are stretched and held in tension by the action of these muscle groups, and the ratio of tension distributed between them causes the length and thickness of the vibrating surface to change with the changing patterns of pitch and intensity. All else is illusion. Since the illusion is created by a particular arrangement of the registration, and the registers respond to specific patterns of pitch and intensity, efforts to develop the technique must be made through adroit manipulation of these tonal elements. To attempt to establish a feeling of 'position,' or sensations of vibration, without having set up a correct registration, is an exercise in futility.

A 'MIXED' REGISTRATION

ONE OF THE primary causes of muscular interference leading to throat constriction and other vocal faults is that the registers become 'mixed.' An improper unification of the registers occurs when the roles of each mechanism become reversed; that is to say, the falsetto becomes overdeveloped and operative too low in the body of the tonal range, while the chest register is thinned out and brought up too high into the middle voice. This has the effect of fattening the upper middle voice range, leaving both outer extremes weak and out of balance. Open-throated singing is absolutely unthinkable as long as the registers remain 'mixed,' as both the arytenoid and crico-thyroid systems are being required to turn against their functional potential and attempt that which they are incapable of executing efficiently. An example which might indicate some of the problems encountered in a 'mixed' registration would be for a pianist to play his repertoire cross-handed rather than the conventional way. Most singers are trained into a mixed registration because their technique is developed out of the one register, or no register, theory.*

SUMMATION

On THE BASIS of the arguments presented in favor of registration the following assumptions now seem justified:
  1. There are two registers: one, the falsetto; the other, the "chest."
  2. Each register must be the product of a separate mechanical (muscular) action.
  3. Each register appears as an automatic reflex to pitch and intensity.
  4. When the falsetto merges with the "chest" register in a coordinate relationship to become the "head" voice, it considerably overlaps the lower, and the two share many notes in common.
  5. Because of the overlap, the voice will often, when reason-

---

*See: Appendix IV; For corrective measures to be taken in curing a 'mixed' registration.

ably well coordinated, appear to be made up of *three* separate divisions.

6. Each tonal area, or division, is recognizable because it is represented by unique textures.

7. Each area owes its special tonal characteristics to the influence of a separated or combined register action.

8. By proper selection of pitch-intensity patterns the registers can be separated or combined on a rather arbitrary basis.

9. Even when operating as a unit, the ratio of registration can still be balanced and set up quite arbitrarily by the instructor, or by the singer himself if he is skilled enough, through proper use of pitch-intensity patterns. (This is only possible when the registers are already quite well-balanced.)

10. The muscular response causing a particular register to predominate is purely involuntary.

11. The interplay of the registers, controllable through pitch and intensity patterns, represents the manipulative device to which the student can respond as an act of *will*.

12. As the reaction of the vocal organs to these simple patterns involves involuntary movement, supposedly inaccessible muscular reflexes can be brought under a very practical kind of control.

13. By skillful use of pitch-intensity patterns the registers can be separated, developed independently, or made to draw together and act as a unit in innumerable relationships involving a balance to be shared between them.

14. These factors, plus temperament, musicality, anatomical structure, and psychological attitudes, are the contributing elements making each voice and personality a unique problem.

While from the foregoing discussion of vocal mechanics we have discovered, among other things, the influence of registration on the vowel, it will be interesting to comment now upon the effect the vowels have on registration.

CHAPTER V

THE VOWEL

Correction of vocal faults is not the exclusive province of the vocal registers. Other agents must be found to assist in reconditioning a badly conditioned reflex. One such agent is the use of primary vowels. Ideally, the articulative needs of the registration and the vowel should be jointly served, and a wisely selected musical exercise will be one which enhances both the purity of the registration and the purity of the vowel at the same time.

Vowels are of particular interest throughout training. Tonal impurities are easily detectable there, as well as misconcepts in the area of pronunciation and quality. However, as vowel distortion lies within the functional process as a whole and not within the vowel proper, purification of the vowel without regard for the condition of the registration or the resonance adjustment will be ineffective. *A vowel will only be as pure as the coordinative process will allow.* Consequently, work on the vowel must move toward two major functional objectives: 1) it must improve the resonance adjustment, *i.e.,* eliminate constrictor tensions, and 2) it must assist in making changes in the registration, whether it be for purposes of separation or unification. The best way to study the behavior patterns of the vowels is to construct an exercise wherein all primary vowels are included so that *they represent the changing factor in an otherwise stable environment.* This can be done quite easily by using a single tone and maintaining a constant level of intensity, while linking the five primary vowels together as 'ah,' 'ay,' 'ee,' 'oh,' and 'oo.'

If a technically well-advanced baritone is asked to sing this exercise on D, below middle C, at a relaxed forte, it will be noticed that the 'oo,' and to a lesser degree the 'ee' vowel, will always require slightly different adjustments. It is perfectly comfortable and easy to articulate the 'ah' with the mouth quite open, and to both feel and hear the rumbling quality of the chest register for the simple reason that it is the dominant mechanism. However, with the 'ee' and the 'oo,' neither the physical position nor the tonal texture remain the same. Moving into the 'ee,' the mouth automatically closes a bit, while at the same time the textural properties of the head voice emerge somewhat stronger. In phonating the 'oo,' the mouth has to close even more, the tonal texture further softens, and the overall feeling is that the tone has come "forward."

Now, suppose the same exercise is performed an octave higher, what then happens? Exactly the same thing—except that the reacting patterns will be more pronounced, with the 'ee' and 'oo' presenting even greater problems. Perhaps not surprisingly, we now find the 'oo' vowel particularly awkward, and it can no longer be well articulated with the mouth in a relatively closed position. The mouth *has* to open more and great care must be taken not to let the vowel degenerate into an 'oh.'

The functional significance of such a study is plain. It should be noticed that when on the upper D the 'oo' tended to open up into an 'oh,' there was a corresponding shift in the tonal texture. The head register quality of the 'oo' when the vowel was kept pure had to modify and disintegrate when the texture changed, as this vowel is incapable of being articulated in the upper tonal regions unless the registers are extremely well coordinated. If the textures of the lower 'oo' and the upper 'oo' are compared, it will be apparent that the vowel changed reflexively to the change in the ratio of registration. The texture which made the 'oo' degenerate into an 'oh' was that of the chest register.

If one were to insist on keeping the vowels pure at all costs so that a real 'oo' is maintained on the upper D even at forte, the singer has no other recourse but to 'cover' the tone. Covering, it is true, will take away the 'too open' quality which makes 'oo' sound like 'oh,' but it also destroys the effectiveness of the resonance adjustment—shutting it off and inducing constrictor tensions. With a covered tone, the effect is one of a 'lid' having been placed on the tone, and consequently, this leads to the ultimate distortion of all the vowels. Covering is a practice to be avoided, except as a temporary expedient.

Returning to the problem of the 'oo,' how can it be made to maintain its purity at forte without recourse to covering? Here we come to the art of the *messa di voce,* the art of balancing the registration so that the ratio of registration for each pitch, intensity, and vowel is in exact proportion to the needs of the musical pattern. Before practicing the *messa di voce,* however, a groundwork must be laid so that it can be executed properly. This groundwork is prepared by employing the same exercise, with one exception. Rather than keeping the intensity constant throughout all five vowels, a slight decrescendo will be made as the 'oo' approaches. The effect of this will be to slack off some of the chest register tension, but not enough to cause the resonance adjustment to collapse. In this way more of the upper register texture will be pulled in. This will immediately eliminate the 'too open' quality of the 'oo' and provide a healthier functional climate. With both registers equitably engaged, pressure can slowly be increased. As long as the unitary function is maintained, there will be no real reason for modifying the vowel any longer.

A striking example illustrating the problem of the 'oo' vowel as it pertains to registration will be found with women's voices. It is impossible for women to sing the 'oo' softly in the chest register, and even when sung loudly it is extremely difficult and tends, as with men's voices, to cause the vowel to modify to 'oh.' So we arrive at four conclusions: 1) that the so-called open vowels are more advantageous when singing in the chest register, 2) that the closed vowels are more adaptable for bringing out the strengths of the head register, 3) that the same reacting patterns occur in both men's and women's voices provided the patterns of pitch, intensity, and the vowel are identical, and 4) that even though the pitch-intensity pattern remains unchanged, the ratio of registration will change with the changing vowel.

The significance of these observations is clear. Registration and adjustments for resonance are not *purely* the result of a functional response to pitch and intensity, although this is primarily so. Equally essential is the assistance of discreetly selected vowels to facilitate the program of register realignment being undertaken.

Needless to say, the possibilities contained within the practice of vowel manipulation are endless. Some of these possibilities have already been explored. In general, a good rule of thumb to remember is this: 'ah' tends to expose the strengths and weaknesses within the registration and affords excellent insights into the type of imbalance present. It is also useful in bringing the chest register into greater prominence. The 'ee' tends to coordinate the registration, but at the same time exposes the weaknesses within the resonance adjustment (constrictor tensions are very easily detectable with the 'ee' vowel). The 'oo' helps to separate the registers, and to coordinate the 'oo' vowel properly is a difficulty not commonly surmounted even by fine artists.

Manipulation of the vowels in order to improve the resonance adjustment and create a better balance of registration is an important teaching tool. Much can be done in this way to bring about a better functional arrangement provided, of course, quality is regarded as vowel quality. The procedure is straightforward. Vowels are used to perfect the purity of the registration, as it is purity of registration (a unified and harmonious coordinative process) that purifies the vowels. Vowel purity and beauty of tone quality are always the results of a healthy functional condition, not causes. Quality is what happens. Function is what makes it happen. Functional freedom alone is responsible for vowel purity and naturalness of tone quality.

CHAPTER VI

ℛESONANCE

ANOTHER vital area of functional interest during training is resonance. Ideally, registration, the vowel, and resonance are equal concerns, no one superseding the others in importance. In actual practice, however, the instruction will often demand a shift in emphasis. With poorly formed voices, registration is always more crucial, because a well-tuned resonance adjustment is impossible when the registration is out of line. On the other hand, when the technique is advanced, the resonance adjustment demands greater attention than the registration, as the efficiency of the registration can be enhanced under certain technical conditions by concentrating on purification of the vowel. During intermediate stages of development there will be a dual emphasis; each lesson will include those exercises designed to correct the registration, as well as those whose intent is to improve the resonance adjustment. As resonance is so important to vocalization, it is essential that it be defined.

Resonance is an immediate amplification of tonal vibrations set in motion by the vocal cords and occurs whenever a cavity is

69

formed whose natural frequency corresponds to the natural frequency of the pitch. The principal cavities involved in forming a chamber of resonance are the oral, the postnasal, and the laryngeal pharynx. The air in these cavities also vibrates in sympathy with the harmonics, or overtones, within the fundamental vibrations determining pitch. This further increases the intensity of the initial source of vibration and reinforces the tone. Tonal resonance, therefore, is the product of a cavity formation which is 'tuned' to the natural frequency of the vibrating cords. Quality is a product of the type of vibration set into motion by the vocal membranes, plus the manner in which overtones are concentrated, dispersed, and augmented. As the quality of sound given off by the vibrating cords alone is inconsequential, cavity resonance of the kind described is an extremely important factor in singing.

Not all of the resonance heard in vocal tone, however, is the product of cavity resonance. In addition, there is forced resonance and sounding board resonance. Forced resonance is a condition in which the initial source of vibration, that is to say, the vibrator, forces a resonator to respond despite the absence of sympathetic tuning. If, for example, a tuning fork is set in motion and touched to a solid object, the initial source of vibration will be reinforced and become louder. Both the piano and the violin operate on the principle of forced resonance. Sounding board resonance has to do with the reflection of tone, as with the echo. The band shell and the tester poised over the pulpit in most churches are good examples of sound reflectors which increase resonance.

It is probable that forced resonance plays a prominent part in vitalizing vocal tone. The solidity of the singer's bone structure and general sturdiness of frame (notable in so many great singers) undoubtedly contribute substantially to tonal vitality and could possibly be said to represent a superior potential. Sounding board resonance merely gives the illusion of amplification, the apparent increase being due to an efficient transfer of vibrations from the vibrating source. It is hardly a factor in singing.

As a vocal concern, resonance is a relatively new development. Earlier instruction centered on but two elements, registration and 'purity of intonation.' A hasty judgment would equate purity of intonation with pitch perception, but, although pitch is a factor, there is more to it than that. Vocal exercises were designed to strengthen the organic response, perfect the registration, and train the ear. But always the tone had to be pure. Pier. Francesco Tosi (1647-1727) made this clear when he wrote, 'Let the master attend with great care to the voice of the scholar, which, whether it be *di petto* or *di testa*, should always come forth neat and clear, without passing through the nose, or being choked in the throat.' He also counseled, 'Let the scholar be obliged to pronounce the vowels distinctly . . . if the fault is not the master's, it is the singers', who are scarce got out of their first lessons' (12). Purity as defined by Tosi implies an unblemished tone quality, and a pure tone is always resonant. Purity of intonation, resonance, and vowel purity are synonymous, each being the reflection of a precisely adjusted co-ordinative process.

Resonance as such was not considered a factor in singing until the early part of the twentieth century. Herbert Witherspoon, a prominent teacher and singer (1873-1935), wrote of 'this comparatively new bugaboo, Resonance.' He further remarked, 'It is an interesting fact that the term nasal resonance I have never found in one of the old books upon the art of singing, either in this country or in Europe' (13). This statement seems to be accurate. A considerable number of books appearing in the nineteenth century deal with the subject of *resonators,* but not resonance. In Garcia's *Hints on Singing,* published in 1894, the subject is not mentioned.

With the arrival on the scene of the music of Wagner and Berlioz (and to a lesser extent, Verdi), it was only natural that greater interest should be shown in resonance. Suddenly, the size of the orchestra increased, with heavy augmentation of the brass. Purity of intonation and registration seemingly needed a reinforcing agent. Volume of tone came to be more highly prized than purity of tone, and functional concerns were shunted aside in favor of concepts given over to tonal 'projection.' Forcing for volume resulted, and strained, effortful vocalization gradually displaced the free-flowing cantilena of the Golden Age of Song. Only a small minority re-

mained faithful to the idea of the immutability of functional laws—
that the correct way to sing is correct for Wagner, Berlioz, and
Schoenberg, as well as for Mozart.

Coincident with the advent of new techniques, abuse of the
mechanism became increasingly common, and the throat doctor
indispensable to a career. The vocal cords were apparently fragile,
and something had to be done. H. Holbrook Curtis suggested
'taking the attack from the cords' and focusing the tone in the
masque (frontal sinuses) in order to relieve the pressure (14).
Ernest White carried this idea a step further and declared, 'The
vocal cords have absolutely nothing whatever to do with voice.
Their function is to *prevent* the passage of air into the mouth, nose
and head.' Consequently, 'registers most positively exist, but are
controlled by making a definite and selective use of the different
cavities or sinuses of the head.' White also quotes Sir Milsom Rees,
who, in lecturing before the British Medical Association at Belfast
(1937), commented, 'These high tones with heavy volume mean
an enormous strain with consequent exhaustion' (15).

As the demand for big voices and voluminous tone increased,
resonance became the focal point of most training methods. The
result was that the core of the functional problem was neglected
in favor of peripheral concerns. Before long, few seemed to remember that the sensations of vibration felt in the head or in the
chest were due to registration.* New systems were devised to 'place
the voice,' the singer being encouraged to feel the vibrations in the
chest and head, to resonate in the sinuses, or to encourage the
'ping' in the tone. These practices have been proven failures, and
such vocal training, instead of solving problems, tends to create
them.

The concept of head and chest resonance, of course, cannot be
taken seriously. The antrim and sinuses are small, nonadjustable

---

*G. B. Lamperti reflected this view when he said, 'The vocal registers are
determined by the different points of resonance of the tone,' and, 'Beauty and
power depend, not simply upon a correct tone-attack, but also upon the resonance
of the voice both in the chest and head.' *Technics of Bel Canto,* Translated by
Theo. Baker, New York: G. Shirmer, Inc., 1905, p. 10.

cavities, heavily damped and not at all suitable for tonal amplification. Furthermore, the openings to the sinuses are so small that these cavities can scarcely be considered a constituent part of the resonance system. William Vennard reports the findings of Warren B. Wooldridge, who, having blocked off entry into the nasal passage with cotton gauze, found no perceptible difference in the characteristics of resonance. Both Vennard and Wooldridge arrive at the same conclusion, finding the entire concept of nasal resonance totally without validity (16). Head resonance should probably be considered an illusion, an illusion created by forced resonance.

Chest resonance is also the product of illusion. In reality, the chest is a cage, not a cavity. Filled with soft, spongy material, it acts as a damper rather than a resonator. The only cavities which are large, adjustable, and possessed of suitable resonating surfaces are the postnasal pharynx, the oral pharynx, and the laryngeal pharynx. Because the larynx houses the vocal cords and surrounds the vocal membranes, and can be positioned, moved, and adjusted, it is ideal for the purpose of resonating tone. The laryngeal pharynx, together with the oral pharynx, represents the functional core of the vocal process. The mouth and the organs of articulation must be considered auxiliaries and, consequently, peripheral concerns. When the coordinative process within the functional core has been made right, all peripheral matters logically fall into place.

The muscles which position the resonators are of little practical interest. The vocal organs are respiratory organs, and muscular activities are involved which extend from the head to the pelvic floor. Some of the muscles can be brought under direct control; most cannot. In any event, the interplay of muscles is so complex that the singer who worries unduly about them is in danger of becoming immobilized. He would be like the centipede who paused to think about which leg moved after which. A positioning process does take place, however, and this process is called a 'resonance adjustment.' To know his voice, the singer must discover those areas in which he can exercise legitimate control over the resonators.

A kinetic 'feel' for resonance is, of course, intuitive and the mark of one who has a talent for singing. But it must be encouraged in a very particular way. In essence, a condition favorable to resonance is operative when the mechanism is held in balanced tension. This means that the larynx is well-positioned in reference to the frequencies set in motion by the vibrating cords, and that the cords themselves are self vibrating—that is to say, virtually independent of breath pressure and responsive solely to those motor impulses from the nervous system which, when the cords are held in balanced tension, produce the vibrations requisite to the sounding of any given pitch (See BREATHING, Chapter XI). To bring this condition about requires an examination of those events which transpire at the precise moment tone is initiated—in the attack.

NASAL RESONANCE vs. NASALITY

THERE IS A fundamental functional distinction to be made between what seems to be nasal resonance and nasality. Nasal resonance (one of the 'mere appearances' referred to by Garcia) finds the throat relatively open with the so-called 'head' register dominant. Under these conditions symptoms of vibration do appear to concentrate in the 'masque,' the area of the sinuses and the antrim. Symptoms, however, must never be confused with causes. Genuine resonance can only be achieved when the technique is open-throated and free of interfering tension, never by 'placing' the tone 'forward' or into the nasal passages. A common pedagogic error is to attempt to establish this freedom through resonance rather than registration.

Nasality is quite another matter. Without exception it is associated with throat constriction, and the proportion of nasality always corresponds exactly to the degree of constriction present in the tone. Few singers possess a technique of singing where the throat is really free and open and nasality is one of the more common vocal faults.

CHAPTER VII

THE ATTACK

Two IMPORTANT factors are involved in the physical process related to vocal tone: 1) the muscular complex which tenses the vocal cords, thus enabling them to meet the requirements of numerous pitch-intensity patterns, and 2) the intrinsic and extrinsic musculature of the laryngeal pharynx which together with the suspensory muscles positioning the larynx, increase the dimensions of the throat cavity to promote resonance. At the inception of vocal tone these forces are set in motion and the movement from relaxation to balanced tension which marks this beginning of the vocal process is called the 'attack.'

The tensing of the vocal cords has been shown to correspond aurally to the mechanics of registration, while adjustments for resonance are made primarily through the creation of vowel forms. Each of these elements, of course, can be made to operate with some degree of independence. Nevertheless, as constituent parts of the total respiratory structure these always interact, with the influence of one directly affecting the activity of the other. Given a

75

certain level of technical proficiency, an improvement in the resonance adjustment will vicariously improve the registration, while
an improved registration will bring about fundamental changes in
the resonance adjustment.

Obviously, many crucial activities center on the attack, for unless
there is a harmonious interplay among all of the forces involved in
Phonation the movement from relaxation to balanced tension will
be imprecise. From a purely physical standpoint, laryngeal behavior is especially significant since the larynx is the 'voice box'
and, as such, the core of the resonating system, as well as the
source of tonal vibration. If training procedures are to be effective,
a way must be found to effect changes in the way the larynx is
positioned without recourse to methods of direct control. Volitional
positioning of the larynx is an extremely dangerous pedagogic procedure and must be avoided at all costs.

Due to the complex of muscles which attach to it (particularly
the supra and infrahyoid groups) the larynx is extremely mobile.
Therefore, it is of the utmost importance that its position during
phonation preserves the natural equilibrium of the total system.
Once this has been accomplishd, the remaining and dependent
elements of the respiratory musculature will be able to meet the
energy demands placed upon it economically. Without a properly
adjusted larynx constrictor tensions are inevitable, the entire system being forced to operate at odds with itself. Correct laryngeal
positioning, therefore, is one of the direct objectives of the vocal
attack, and represents an act of physical skill without which the
voice cannot emerge freely.

A consideration of laryngeal activity, or the throat as an active
participant in the phonative process, is an area of concern care-
fully avoided, both in theory and in practice, by a majority of
those who teach voice at the present time. It is true, commands
are frequently given to 'open the throat,' but the instruction is
never implemented with practical suggestions. More commonly
the student is told to 'get the tone out of the throat,' to 'relax the

throat,' or to 'bring the tone forward,' each directive transparently working *away* from a reasonable solution to the problem. Rarely is an effort made to improve the physical adjustment assumed by the larynx as it moves to meet the demands of a melodic pattern in terms of functional requirements.

Yet this has not always been so. Late in the nineteenth century, John Howard, a practicing physician as well as a prominent voice teacher, offered substantial evidence to support his belief that the larynx was the primary resonator of vocal tone, as well as being the source of vibratory impulses (17). Many years before Tosi spoke of the *voce di testa,* the voice of the head, which, paradoxically, 'comes more from the throat than from the breast,' and the falsetto, a 'feigned voice,' which he declared to be 'entirely formed in the throat' (12). Shortly before the turn of the last century, Garcia advocated 'keeping the larynx firm' as a solution to the problem of tonal unsteadiness (8). Another source, William Earl Brown, a pupil of G. B. Lamperti (1840-1910), quotes his teacher as saying, 'Tone is "felt" in the head, though caused in the throat' (18). For many years, also, the *voce di gola* or voice of the throat, enjoyed a prominent place in vocal nomenclature. Isaac Nathan (1792-1864) ascribed this to the falsetto, and without doubt this expression also represents a concept having to do with laryngeal positioning.

Another Lamperti pupil keenly aware of the need for a correct laryngeal adjustment was a teacher with the unlikely name of William Shakespeare (1849-1931). He also shed interesting light on the now widely accepted doctrine of voice 'placement.' 'In order to produce any note in fullness and purity of tone,' he states, 'it is necessary to place or balance the larynx over the breath and retain it in its appropriate position'. Shakespeare was also perceptive enough to recognize the close connection between the 'placing' muscles of the larynx and the vocal registers. To quote again, 'Thus the registers seem to be influenced by different sets of placing muscles; the latter through interchange of action balance the larynx in the exact position necessary to any tone, high or low, loud or soft; simultaneously, the muscles inside bring about the infinite and remarkable modifications in the length and breadth of the vibrating cords to which reference has already been made' (19).

If we address ourselves to the problem of laryngeal function and the positioning processes that naturally take place, we are again struck by the fact that movement is involved. Strangely enough, it is the motility of the larynx, its ability to assume various positions, that is so often overlooked. It is due to this potential that the concept of 'positioning,' of 'holding' a resonance adjustment, and the need for 'resistance' become so important.

Serious teachers of voice are deeply indebted to Frederick Husler for clarifying this aspect of technique. In his book, *Singing: The Physical Nature of the Vocal Organ,* he describes the position of the larynx as being sustained by a type of elastic scaffolding. Within this scaffolding, the mechanism is flexibly suspended and held in balanced tension by an opposed muscular system described as 'elevators' and 'depressors.' Involved are the thyro-hyoid and stylo-pharyngeal muscles, (which raise the larynx) and the sterno-thyroid and crico-pharyngeal muscles (which draw the larynx downward). The palato-laryngeal muscle also participates in this elevating process as, obviously, the soft palate forms an integral part of the resonating system, as well as being a primary factor in vowel formation.

Directionally speaking, the term 'elevator' and 'depressor' are somewhat misleading, implying that the movement of the larynx is purely up and down. This is not quite true. The thyro-hyoid, a paired muscle which elevates the laryngeal position, draws directly upward toward twelve o'clock. Its antagonist, the sterno-thyroid, also a paired muscle, pulls in the opposite direction, but more towards seven o'clock. The sterno-pharyngeal muscle, an elevator, pulls toward one o'clock, while the crico-pharyngeal muscle moves in the direction of three o'clock.

FIGURE IV

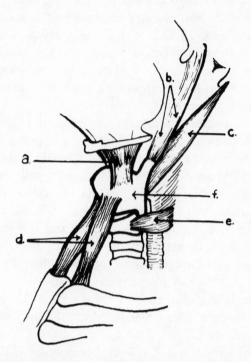

FIG. IV. Suspensory mechanism. a) thyro-hyoid, b) muscles of the palate, c) stylo-pharyngeal, d) sterno thyroid, e) crico-pharyngeal. Each of these geal. Each of these muscles plays an important role in adjusting the larynx so as to enable it to function as a primary resonator. (diagram after Husler)

A brief glance at the directional pulls of the muscles comprising the suspensory mechanism (shown in Figure IV) clearly indicates the positioning process as it affects the larynx. To quote Mr. Husler, 'The various paired muscles of the suspensory mechanism pull on the larynx in four different directions. Each of these directional pulls is able to alter substantially the shape and the degree of tension of the vocal folds, and of the laryngeal cavity above. Each one changes the tonal character of the voice, its possible variations being almost limitless' (20).

In this statement Husler touches upon the core of the functional process, in that 1) through the intricate interpositioning of the suspensory muscles the essential character of a resonance adjustment is determined, 2) due to a correct laryngeal suspension all techniques of breathing become subordinate considerations, and 3) when the suspensory mechanism is in equilibrium the vocal registers will respond by improving their alignment, through a self-regenerative process.

With the suspensory mechanism capable of pulling the larynx in four different directions, it is clear that the possibilities of inter-adjustment are indeed without limit. Of special interest is the action of the sterna-thyroid because its contraction pulls on the thyroid cartilage. This further complicates the movement of the larynx, in that it permits it to be tilted somewhat forward and backward. From a functional standpoint, it is here that the varying degrees of open and closed-throated singing find their point of origin. To speak of open and closed-throated singing, therefore, is to make direct reference to a physiological condition.

The larynx is the source of all vocal tone. The physical properties of the singing voice originate there, the musculature responsible for registration is housed there, the primary source of resonance is to be found within it, and it is the member to which the suspensory muscles attach themselves in order to connect the upper part of the respiratory system to the skeletal framework. It seems beyond dispute, therefore, that the most important factor in vocal training is the development of the muscular system which controls the opening of the laryngeal pharynx. The essential purpose of the attack is to correctly innervate these muscles. A clean attack is one in which the laryngeal suspension is precise and 'well-tuned' to the fundamental. It is synonymous with open-throated singing.*

The achievement of an open-throated resonance adjustment is most difficult. Those who manage to sing in such a manner usually do so because nature has been kind, which is why the expression

---

*Singing with an open throat must not be taken to mean that the laryngeal and oral pharynx are to be volitionally widened. To act on the mechanism in such a way leads to throat stiffness. The throat may be said to be open when the larynx is well-positioned and there are no constricting tensions present.

'she is an extremely gifted singer' rings so true in a literal sense. Few achieve this distinction. Singing with an open throat means but one thing: that the vocal function operates in conformity with the laws of physiology, and any deviation from those laws must be very slight if constrictor tensions are not to intrude. An equilibrium of this kind requires tremendous sensitivity—a sensitivity which unites the conceptual, the physical and the emotional, holding them in an exquisitely delicate and precise relationship. Openthroated singing is the goal of vocal pedagogy, however, not the problem. The physical problem is caused by a poorly suspended larynx, the root of all throat constriction.

A correctly suspended larynx affords the singer many technical advantages. It provides a natural and beautiful tone quality, causes the voice to 'ring,' assures tonal steadiness, ease, and flexibility. It also gives to the softest tones a 'carrying power' that would otherwise be absent. It further creates the illusion of tones being 'well-supported' and 'well-focused.' Without a correctly suspended larynx these advantages would be dissipated, with the result that artistic goals would have to be compromised.

THROAT CONSTRICTION

THE attack, as we have seen, is a positioning process which draws the vocal cords into tension for pitch and adjusts the larynx and the pharyngeal cavities lying above to ensure tonal resonance. Also involved is a complex network of muscles which permit the articulation of consonants, without which there would be no language. All of these are overlaid functions, the primary organic purpose being respiration. The vocal problem is further complicated by the fact that the respiratory organs naturally perform another basic function which is swallowing.

It is the act of swallowing which helps make vocalization so difficult. Swallowing occurs reflexively and the muscles governing mastication and ingestion interfere all too easily with the vocal process. The dynamic movement in peristalsis is not muscular ex-

pansion, but contraction. In opposition to this is the vocal need
for a positioning process in which the ideal adjustments made for
pitch, intensity, and the vowel will maintain the throat in an open
position for a considerable period of time. Unfortunately for the
singer, peristaltic action is also associated with the crico-thyroids
which are directly involved in stretching the vocal cords for pitch.
Thus, the laryngeal muscles responsible for phonation may seem
to be more intimately associated with a natural movement which
closes the throat than they are with an opening action. In short,
it is easier for the student to identify kinetically with a constricting
movement than with one which opens the throat.

In a faulty laryngeal suspension, the muscles of the tongue as
well as a large number of swallowing muscles (the upper or superior constrictor, the middle constrictor, and the lower or inferior
constrictor) come into tension to reduce the size of the throat
cavity. This narrowing of the pharyngeal tract causes the emer-
gent sounds to possess a quality commonly known as 'throatiness.'
Throatiness distorts the purity of the tone quality, brings on early
vocal fatigue, causes the voice to become tremulous, and interferes
with the free movement of the articulatory processes. Each of
these shortcomings betrays the presence of constrictor tension.

Throat constriction is a universal vocal problem. The purely
physical aspects of this problem may be attributed to the virtually
limitless movement potential of the muscles comprising the respiratory system. Out of this vast potential there is but one adjustment
for each pitch, intensity and vowel pattern which will yield a perfect tone, all others ranging anywhere from highly efficient to totally
ineffectual. The degree to which the vocal organs and their auxiliary musculature are correctly innervated will determine the degree
to which the technique has achieved a status of functional health.

The need to position the larynx lies at the heart of the vocal
process, and making contact with a dynamic laryngeal poise is a
problem basic to all but the exceptional singer. Among other
factors which make the problem excessively difficult is this: the
positioning process must be accomplished without recourse to
methods of direct control. Denied a direct mode of access, what

procedures then are practical, and what means can be devised for influencing the internal and external musculature of the larynx so that they, together with their auxiliary and dependent muscles, can be effectively coordinated? If a satisfactory answer to this question can be found we will have at our disposal the necessary means for restructuring vocal techniques which would otherwise remain bound and restricted.

Shakespear's suggestion to 'place or balance the larynx over the breath and retain it in its appropriate position,' although loosely phrased, gives the appearance of being helpful, but it is deceptive. From a functional standpoint his use of the word 'place' is misleading. It implies volitional effort, and the suspensory muscles of the larynx are not subject to legitimate volitional control. It is true, the throat can be volitionally opened, but *after* an open-throated technique has become a reality. For those whose throats are not yet open, who are groping toward an experience they have not yet experienced, such a proposition is futile. Volitional attempts to influence and control involuntary muscular activities will inevitably prove self-defeating. A desirable solution must be sought elsewhere if the larynx is to be made to participate effectively in the phonative process.

SELF-REGULATION

No PROCEDURE for positioning the larynx is valid unless it engages those principles which govern natural movement and recognizes the inherent tendency of an organism to regulate itself. We have already seen how natural movement can be encouraged through the mechanics of registration and its associated disciplines. We must now apply this same logic to the problem of laryngeal suspension. This cannot be done without some understanding of the general nature of self-regulation.

Self-regulation is the inherent ability of an organism to recognize, and respond favorably to, a congenial environment. In singing, the external environment consists of primary musical elements.

This idea, whether it be a simple scale or a complete melody, constitutes, in effect, a stimulus to which the vocal organs respond. If the stimulus (environment) is such that it promotes healthy reflexive movement, then the respiratory organs will adapt successfully to the vocal process. When a stimulus is projected which violates functional laws, natural movement gives way to restricted movement and the laryngeal musculature must be *made* to move. Forcing movement makes the voice sluggish and dissipates energy.

Self-regulation is an intrinsic characteristic of natural movement and can best be described as vocal self-interest. When exercises selected during training are thoughtfully constructed, the organic system will move spontaneously and willingly—it perceives that its best interests are being served and responds accordingly. The tendency of an organism to regulate itself, therefore, is simply a response which indicates that the demands placed upon it can be successfully carried out within the framework of its movement potential. Organic systems may thus be said to be capable of recognizing a distinction between use and abuse.

One of the continuing fascinations of functional training is listening to the vocal organs saying, in their own way, 'yea' and 'nay' to the procedures to which they have been made to adapt.* In a hostile environment (when demands in the form of exercise patterns are made which run counter to natural movement) the organs stiffen, yielding visible as well as aural evidence of the abuse to which they are being subjected. When environmental influences improve, visible signs of wrong tension disappear; there is greater ease of production, superior tone quality, an extension of the vocal compass, and less fatigue. The assumption that an organic system is disposed to regulate itself wisely if permitted to do so is supportable by a wealth of concrete evidence.

Unless correction of a vocal problem is based upon an understanding of self-regulation, training procedures run the risk of losing contact with functional naturalness. Such a failure precludes any hope of inducing a correct laryngeal suspension and

---

*Music said to be 'vocal' is an example of a congenial climate which helps the mechanism function at its best.

leads to serious errors, as to both procedure and theory. Furthermore, an absence of contact with natural organic movement leaves tonal concepts at the mercy of cultural attitudes, teacher-imposed taste, a vocal fashion growing out of a prevailing emotional climate, conditioning, and the often deleterious influence of linguistic and ethnic peculiarities.

Opposed to this, an understanding of the procedures associated with self-regulation, together with a firm grasp of the principles governing registration and adjustments for resonance, will encourage natural and functionally correct response patterns which transcend limitations of this description. In this process, if the vocal exercises selected represent the kind of 'exercise' the vocal organs require to achieve greater stabilization, the singer's instinct for creative expression should be awakened. With both knowledge and instinct working for him he should then be ready, under instruction, to attempt the rather formidable task of positioning the larynx without running the risk of constricting the throat.

CHAPTER VIII

EXERCISES FOR

LARYNGEAL SUSPENSION

THE PURPOSE of a vocal exercise is to encourage naturalness of movement, to remove muscular blockages, to strengthen that which is correct, to develop and properly integrate the vocal registers, and to effectively position the larynx so that it provides the open-throated resonance so essential to good singing. If this can be accomplished the movement of the vocal muscles will be efficient and economical.

Stimulating the vocal muscles so that the throat will open is a special responsibility. If one is to get at the functional core of the vocal apparatus he must know what scale patterns to select, when and how to project them, and why they can be expected to work. Each exercise must be tailored to fit the individual and, while certain patterns apply to all, nevertheless each must be used at the right time under the right circumstances.

When exercise patterns are chosen wisely they will, for the more advanced student, improve both the registration and the laryngeal suspension. This, in turn, should open the throat. A

number of exercises for realigning the registration have already
been suggested. Listed below are some of those which experience
has shown to be useful for innervating the suspensory muscles so
that they will position themselves reflexively in an appropriate
manner. Apart from those already discussed in conjunction with
registration, there are:

> the staccato
> the octave jump with reiterated upper note
> arpeggii without tonal pulse
> the trill on major thirds
> the octave jump with a rapid triad added to the upper note
> an exercise which I call the 'trombone slide.'

Used with understanding, these exercises should help the singer
gain a kinetic sense of laryngeal function. They should lead him,
without recourse to mechanistic methods, to an awareness of his
throat as a vital participant in the phonative process.

THE STACCATO: Staccato effects used for the purpose of
promoting healthy laryngeal action are quite unlike those normally
heard in agility exercises. A chest register balance must be encouraged at the expense of lightness, and the exercise performed
with considerable vigor. The type of laryngeal response looked for
is that experienced in a hearty belly laugh, as in 'Ha-Ha-Ha,' but
without the aspirate. Conscious throat action must be avoided in
favor of spontaneity until such time as the correct functional response registers as a concrete impression, conceptual and physical,
to which the singer can respond on a volitional basis. The most
appropirate musical figure for this exercise is the repeated arpeggio; the vowels, 'ah', and 'ee.'

VARIATIONS: Many variations of the staccato attack may
be used. Those immediately at hand are:

1. A repeated arpeggio, the first full arpeggio sung staccato,
   the first half of the second sung staccato with the octave sustained, then finished legato.

2. A repeated arpeggio, each half of the figure sung alternately
   staccato and legato.

3. The single arpeggio sung legato with the upper note a reiterated staccato.
4. A staccato arpeggio with a trill introduced on the upper note.
5. With women's voices, an inverted arpeggio sung legato with
   added thirds and fifths may be used. The topmost note
   must combine the cleanliness of the staccato attack with the
   legato phrase. Usually it is advisable to conclude this exercise by adding the chest register on the tonic.
6. With male voices the staccato arpeggii may also be practiced
   in the falsetto. This exercise should start on G, above middle
   C, and range from E flat, above high C, to G, below middle
   C. 'Ah' and 'ee' are the most suitable vowels, although
   occasionally the 'oo' is helpful.

N.B. All staccato effects must be initiated from the larynx and
not by a push from the diaphragm! To further isolate the
laryngeal function and develop a 'feel' for its movement
potential keep the body and head motionless!

THE OCTAVE JUMP: The octave jump as an exercise to
promote a full-throated laryngeal action is identical to that used
when separating and/or combining the registers, except that the
upper note is reiterated several times in the manner of the staccato
attack described above. Garcia employed a similar exercise for
articulating the coup de glotte, suggesting as a preliminary stage
the use of a very rapid appoggiatura of less than a semi-tone (8).
For example, with higher.voices, if the octave jump is in the key of
F, the upper F would be approached from the E, immediately
below. The effect of this is to encourage greater chest register
participation and, consequently, more throat action. Having induced a healthy and vigorous laryngeal response, the appoggiatura
must then be eliminated. At this stage of development the upper
tone should be started as though it were a gentle staccato, an
attack which can be effectively transformed into a sustained tone.

It is my belief that Garcia's *coup de glotte* and Husler's concept
of laryngeal suspension are one and the same. In any event, experience has shown that the octave jump, either with or without
the appoggiatura, will provide the singer with a very strong kinetic

sense of laryngeal action. It must be reemphasized, however, that the aspirate is to be studiously avoided. Breath flow is to be checked, not released.

In connection with Garcia's use of the appoggiatura, it is interesting to note that the habit of scooping into which so many fine singers have sometimes degenerated may simply be a careless execution of the *coup de glotte.* Certainly it appears to be an attempt to initiate a familiar laryngeal action with the intent of opening the throat and gaining security and control.

After the singer has become aware of a correct laryngeal position the next step is to take some of the weight out of the voice and make it more lyric. This can be done by singing firmly on the tonic (to ensure an open-throated resonance adjustment, which means that the chest register will be somewhat dominant) then attacking the upper tone, keeping the same resonance adjustment, but a lowered level of intensity. By having lowered the intensity of the upper note, the strength of the chest register will lessen at which point the head voice will be more inclined to take over.

From this exercise the messa di voce can also be developed. Simply take the head voice tone at the reduced level of volume and swell upon it. The result should be a forte in which the proportion of head register to chest register will be equitably maintained.

STRAIGHT TONES: Occasionally a run of arpeggii sung without tonal pulse can be extremely helpful in gaining a sense of laryngeal resistance. This exercise also serves another useful purpose—it helps get around the singer's aesthetic concept, which, being subjective, is inevitably a misconcept. Over the years the tonal pulse, however inoffensive it may be, has become part of the singer's subconscious aesthetic. As such, it is also part of his technical problem. And it is a difficult problem because he rarely sees it in those terms.

Straight tones without vibrato are very effective for driving out a wrong tonal pulse. As it is against nature to sing 'straight' tones, a new pulse will ultimately tend to emerge out of the straightness. A double advantage is gained here: new conceptual images can be formed and developed, while at the same time the functional response of the vocal organs will have been improved. A curious fact about this exercise is that it tends to eliminate the drag of the chest register and introduce considerably more head register response. Considerable skill is required to exploit the straight tone, as the conditions must be just right. An inopportune attempt, or a faulty execution, can spell disaster.

TRILL ON MAJOR THIRDS: The trill on major thirds serves a dual purpose. It encourages a sense of laryngeal action, and it assists the rotary action of the registration. The ideal scale pattern to be employed is the octave arpeggio with an added third.

Little difficulty should be experienced with this exercise as it almost works itself. Commencing with the tonic, and riding with the sweep of the phrase, the rhythmic elan should be such as to cause the register balance between the octave and the third above to regulate itself freely. At the same time, the singer must be careful to maintain a constant resonance adjustment so as not to disturb the laryngeal suspension. If successful, he will discover the answer to a most curious paradox—how to permit movement (reflex activity on the part of involuntary muscles) without moving (while rendering passive all volitionally controllable muscles). The effect of this exercise will be to introduce a clear mental picture, *after the event,* of the manner in which the vocal registers rebalance themselves in response to a changing pitch pattern, while at the same time the suspensory muscles (the resonance adjustment) are held in a fixed position, free of grip or stiffness. Occasionally, an arpeggio with a trill between the fifth and the upper octave will serve the same purpose.

THE 'TROMBONE SLIDE': It seems unlikely that one of the most distressing vocal faults, slurring, can be turned to good advantage in building a vocal technique, yet such is the case. There is an important difference, however, between a slur and the vocal imitation of the trombone slide. In a slur the resonance adjustment between the lower and the upper notes is not maintained, whereas in the trombone slide, it is.

The execution of the trombone slide is quite simple. It must be done by slurring from octave to octave and, despite the fact that a slight change of register balance will be detectable on the upper notes, a homogeneous quality must be preserved. That is to say, there must be no detachment, however slight, between the registers as they rotate from one extreme of pitch range to the other. Neither must there be a tonal pulse, and the effect is precisely that heard in a trombone slide. If well executed, this exercise will afford the singer a strong sense of healthy, invigorating laryngeal participation. Another benefit will be the element of release. The feeling of 'letting go' is intrinsic to this exercise, since the free, spontaneous slide through the phrase cancels out the common tendency to 'grip' and 'control' the organic adjustments.

Once the singer has experienced a sense of proper laryngeal activity, he should encounter little difficulty in applying this feeling of freedom to a legato phrase featuring precise intervals. He should now be able to make a clear distinction between work and struggle, between the right and the wrong kind of resistance to the energy thrust being generated. This, in turn, should lead to an awareness of the significance of equilibrium, of a balance between the outward expenditure of energy and the 'holding' action provided by a proper laryngeal suspension. In short, the singer should now be able to energize his vocal organs properly.

All of the foregoing exercises, together with those designed to rebalance the registration, can be useful in establishing an open-throated resonance adjustment. Unless a strong sense of healthy laryngeal suspension can be engendered at the moment of attack the singer really hasn't much to work with. If he sings vigorously he will resort to pushing. If he sings lightly he will reinforce those constrictor tensions already eating away at the foundations of his technique. Healthy, open-throated singing, with its unique quality and durability, is impossible unless the larynx is positioned properly.

To 'place the larynx over the breath,' as Shakespeare rather quaintly described a resonance adjustment, requires an 'interchange of action which balances the larynx in the exact position necessary to any tone, high or low, loud or soft.' The exercises listed above should help the muscles responsible for this positioning process to function in a manner consonant with their lawful order. None of the exercises is mechanistic, and to treat them as such would be to miss the point at issue. Exercises should be spontaneously (rhythmically) executed in order to avoid self-consciousness, as contact cannot be made with involuntary responses while negative tensions prevail. When utilized in this manner, these and similar exercises should go a long way toward opening the throat and creating a condition in which tone quality will be natural and the resonance genuine and unforced.

It is important to note at this point that no exercise posseses intrinsic value. Without the teacher's trained 'ear,' his knowledge of functional mechanics, his skill in being able to equate the sound that is heard with its corresponding functional condition, together with his ability to empathize, any, or all, exercises employed may prove to be of negative value, or even damaging. The human voice is a reflection of the human personality—nothing always works, and sometimes that which does work seems totally inexplicable. By remaining open to all possibilities, however, a correct positioning of the larynx can be managed.

The importance of the suspensory muscles to correct vocalization cannot be overestimated. When properly adjusted they determine the effectiveness of the resonance adjustment, improve the registration, conserve the breath, free the articulatory processes, and overall, cause each phase of the peripheral musculature to perform more effectively. Another far-reaching benefit of a correct laryngeal suspension is that, as an integral part of the respiratory system, it reflexively engages all of the muscles comprising that system, holding them in balanced tension. Correct laryngeal activity links the throat, the respiratory system, and the entire body into a harmonious functional relationship. The unifying element of this relationship is the attack.

CHAPTER IX

FUNCTIONAL ANALYSIS

TONE quality is the end result of a mental and physical process and, consequently, subject to analysis on both levels. As all tone qualities are a composite of tonal textures which originate in registration and adjustments made for resonance, it is possible for the trained ear to recognize technical difficulties at their source and set in motion the necessary procedures for correcting them. The following table (Figure V) lists a wide variety of functional possibilities and indicates how they influence quality.

All three of the categories mentioned below are of special interest. Each is important functionally, and most are subject to modification and change. By selecting one category out of each group it is possible to assess with considerable accuracy the nature of the vocal faults either present or absent. The first category has been planned to indicate the seven most common physical arrangements of the registration. These arrangements are:

1. A state of perfect coordination where both registers have

FIGURE V
TONAL TEXTURES AND THEIR SOURCES

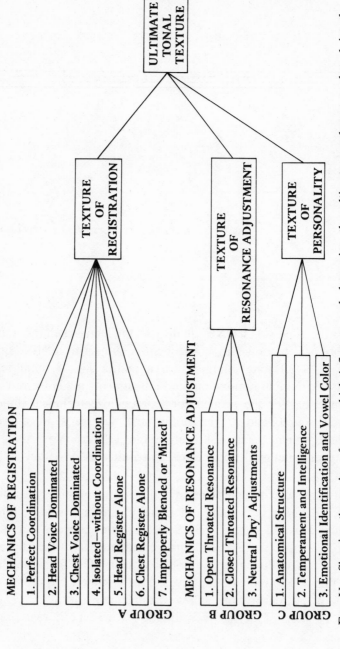

Fig. V. Showing the various factors which influence and determine the ultimate tonal texture heard by the listener.

been fully developed and smoothly joined. This occurs but rarely.

2. A divided registration whose action is dominated by the UPPER register or 'head' voice.

3. A divided registration whose action is dominated by the lower register, or 'chest' voice.

4. A condition where both registers are used, but with an audible gap separating them. In this arrangement the registers are often so widely separated as to prohibit free passage from one to the other. This makes singing difficult, if not impossible. If the gap is narrow the technique is ready to move into either one of the higher categories. Of all the categories listed this is the broadest and within it the technical status of the singer can be anywhere from the primitive to the fairly advanced.

5. A condition where the falsetto, or 'head' voice, is used alone while the lower register is excluded entirely from discernable participation. This situation is not likely to be encountered with the male voice.

6. A condition where the 'chest' register is used exclusively, while the 'head' register is neglected. This condition is common to the male voice, less so to the female unless she is 'belting out' popular songs.

7. An improper blending or 'mixture' of the registers in which they have been smoothly joined in a wrong balance. This introduces muscular conflicts which can never be resolved without disengaging the registration. The problem here is that the procedures necessary to the correction of one fault will often intensify another, making a just solution impossible. For example, in order to break down the constrictor tensions always associated with a mixed registration, the chest register must be reestablished in its rightful place. But the vigor required to make this mechanism operative will, if the mixture of the registers is too severe, merely serve to fortify the very constrictions it is supposed to dislodge. Thus, what is essential to a successful realignment of

the registration will often bring about a worsening of the resonance adjustment. For some types of mixed registration, therefore, no solution exists. Certain mixtures, however, notably those allied with the average lyric tenor, often mistakenly referred to as the Bel Canto type, are functional to a degree and, with patience, subject to correction.

Each of the seven mechanical arrangements of the registration described is accompanied by representative textures which may easily be recognized as belonging to either the 'head' register, the 'chest' register, or some combination of the two. In addition, there are the resonance adjustments made for tonal amplification, and these fall into three basic categories:

1. An ideal adjustment where a condition of precise, 'open-throated' resonance has been established.
2. A reversal of this ideal adjustment, during which time constrictor tensions take over and the tonal resonance becomes 'throaty.'
3. A neutral adjustment having a 'dry' tonal quality. Where 'dryness' of tone is a problem the throat is neither actively 'open' nor actively 'closed.' The absence of vitality in 'dry' voices always indicates a position of formlessness in the resonance adjustment. Without exception the registration will also be faulty.

All of the classifications so far mentioned represent the several types of coordinative processes commonly met with as the vocal organs respond to pitch-intensity patterns and the vowel. From this it follows that tone quality, i.e., vowel quality and *timbre,* must in effect be a repository for whatever textural contribution each category of mechanical response has to offer. Evidence may always be found within the tone quality to show the extent of those textural modifications introduced by the character of the coordinative arrangement prevalent at a given moment. Beyond these factors, others must be considered. They are:

1. The influence of individual anatomical structure. This is an unchangeable factor, but nonetheless plays an important

role in determining the natural tessitura and textural properties of the voice.

2. The influence of temperament. It goes without saying that
   qualities of temperament and intelligence play an important
   role in the infusion of individual quality characteristics which
   make every voice distinctive and individual.

3. The influence on texture of the quality of emotional identification. 'Coloring' the vowel to dramatize the emotional
   import of the lyrics is one of the chief interpretive devices
   at the singer's disposal.

Most of the subtle adjustments made in 'coloring' the vowel are
emotionally oriented. They take position as a response to feelings
commonly associated with vocal literature such as love, anger, fear,
disdain, happiness, longing, grief, jealousy, and the like. However,
before the ultimate purpose of singing is confronted, which is to
convey with great sensitivity a full range of emotional experience
episodically, the pure joy of making sound for its own sake must
be developed. How the singer relates to this is another important
aspect of vocal color, for the *quality* of his identification, his
response *to* feeling *through* feeling, will in the long run establish
his value as an artist.

The capacity of the singer to relate with emotional sensitivity
depends upon functional freedom. Unless the registration is properly balanced and the resonance adjustments well-formed, vowel
'coloring' must always be contrived and artificial. Functional freedom *awakens* feelings, and when this happens it is not necessary
to 'put' feeling into anything. It is there.

From what has been said, the tonal textures heard as the end
product of a singer's technique can be evaluated with some accuracy simply by understanding the mechanical relationships between
cause and effect, i.e., the effect upon the tonal texture of the anatomical structure, temperament and vowel coloring, together with
the coordinative pattern of response offered by the registers and
the resonance adjustment. When these elements are placed in
their proper perspective a real understanding of the vocal function
will have been gained.

CHAPTER X

CONCEPT AND FUNCTION

THE PRACTICAL working out of any train-
ing program must begin with the mental concept. In this respect
every singer is a duality. On the one hand he possesses a conceptual viewpoint which, while reflecting personal taste, may nevertheless be considered objective. That is to say, in the absence of
muscular involvement, as a listener, he can often make relatively
dispassionate judgments. On the other hand, as a *doer* he enter-
tains a conceptual viewpoint which is purely subjective. Each of
these viewpoints is somewhat distorted and at variance not only
with one another, but with functional logic as well.

For the singer, objective judgments are of lesser importance
than those which are subjective. Training must begin, therefore,
with an effort to improve and perfect subjective concepts. In this
program the student must be taught what to listen for; then, when
he becomes capable of making right value judgments among aural
phenomena and functional laws, both objective and subjective
judgments will have been brought into agreement. The questions

98

that arise are: what influences have been at work in the development of conceptual attitudes, and what does one learn to listen for?

To answer the second question first, intelligent listening requires of the singer two things: 1) that he forget 'quality' and focus his attention on purifying the vowel, and 2) that he learns to associate numerous tonal textures with their causative factors, i.e., registration and resonance adjustments. Once this kind of tonal discernment has been mastered all barriers between theory and practice should no longer exist. Teaching materials then become both tangible and workable. More will be said about this shortly.

To return to the first question, it is hardly necessary to point out that many and diverse influences play a part in the development of a vocal self-image, and that identification begins early in infancy. Depending upon the freedom with which the body responds, the coordinative pattern evolving during growth into adulthood will unite expressive goals, talent, intelligence and status of emotional health into an entity, an entity which from earliest childhood becomes frozen into a concept of the self. Thus, by the time vocal study is begun, the student recognizes and accepts certain tonal qualities as being peculiarly his own; the sounds associated with the coordinative response with which he has lived so long a time become fixed in his mind as 'his quality.' What he only vaguely realizes, however, is the extent to which his conceptual image has to be altered in order to meet in agreement with nature's laws. To the degree to which he is capable of adapting to new conceptual images, to that degree will radical technical improvement be made.

There are, then, three separate aspects of the mental concept to be considered during training: 1) a concept which has been formed through personal identification of long standing, 2) an automatic pre-forming of this concept at the outset of phonation in order to duplicate an experience which, at best, is merely habitual and familiar, and 3) the need to re-form this concept so as to provoke changes in the coordinative response of the laryngeal and pharyngeal muscles engaged.

In adapting to new conceptual images the question arises as to how this is to be managed. Adapt to what? How can anyone be expected to adapt to a new conceptual image, or form an unfamiliar coordinative pattern, when neither the physical adjustment nor its equivalent expression in tone quality has fallen within his experience? In other words, how can anyone sing a tone quality of which he has had no prior vision or knowledge? This problem is not atypical, for it is common to almost every teaching situation; the tone quality looked for during training is the tone quality neither the student nor the teacher has yet been privileged to hear. Let us see if there is not some way for this dilemma to be resolved.

When they have not been placed under artificial restraint, phonative processes will react spontaneously. In preceding chapters two important facts were disclosed in reference to this: 1) that pitch-intensity patterns of a specific design and arrangement coincide with the phenomenon of registration, and 2) that resonance adjustments are automatic reflexes made in response to the vowel. Each of these, in turn, are influenced by concepts concerning expressive goals, i.e., aesthetic and emotional attitudes toward 'quality.'

Many pedagogic opportunities exist because of the involuntary nature of the laryngeal muscles participating in phonation. Since the vocal organs react in a predictable manner to pitch and intensity, it consequently is possible to change habitual patterns of response by proper manipulation of these elements. Under skillful supervision, unfamiliar qualities should emerge, qualities which have not been pre-conceptualized and which should represent a radical departure from aesthetic goals entertained prior to the moment of singing.

A practical means for developing new conceptual images is then available. The student need only concentrate on the pitch, intensity and vowel patterns projected by the teacher and respond freely without regard to aesthetic goals. Quality expressed in terms of 'my quality,' 'forwardness,' 'point,' 'ping,' 'nasal resonance,' or any other imagery that interferes with the vocal process, must be ruthlessly discarded from the pre-concept. Left unencumbered by outer-imposed disciplines, the vocal organs can then be expected to react in a manner more in keeping with their functional potential. Through reliance upon natural movement, changes in quality and in the textural properties of the registration will occur, changes *which will be anticipated by the teacher, but not by the student.*

It should now be apparent that a knowledge of registration provides the necessary means for correcting any and all technical situations, as well as providing a basis for a revision of concepts. What seems increasingly obvious is the need to reject culturally and emotionally derived attitudes associated with taste. Natural quality, a product of natural movement, depends upon evaluations which must agree not with taste, but with nature's laws. This means that objective and subjective concepts are to be brought into agreement not only with each other, but with the functional logic by which the vocal organs are governed.

CHAPTER XI

BREATHING

SINCE preparation for the phonative process involves the act of breathing, a consideration of the effect of that act on the laryngeal musculature is in order. The result of such a consideration will be to expose a direct functional contradiction between the act of natural breathing and the response of the vocal cords as they position themselves to meet the requirements of pitch and intensity (See: Fig. I).

In normal respiration the vocal cords open reflexively with each inhalation and exhalation performed. They close but for a brief moment whenever there is a shift from one action to the other. Inasmuch as the phonative act requires an approximation of the cords, so that their edges run parallel without touching, it is obvious that this process is subverted whenever inspiratory or expiratory muscles come into tension. The specific nature of the problem is that natural breathing forces the cords apart when, in order to vibrate properly, they should be together.

From what is now known of functional mechanics it is clear that

102

the proper closing of the glottal space is caused by a correctly balanced registration. When the muscles drawing the cords into tension for the required pitch and intensity coordinate effectively, the end result finds the edges of the cords running parallel. No technique of breathing is capable of closing the glottal space properly unless the registers are well-balanced. One can save breath by constricting the throat when the registers are out of phase, but not through a legitimate closing of the glottis. The pedagogic problem is to find some means for neutralizing both inspiratory and expiratory tension so that the act of breathing is not permitted to interfere with the registration, and to do so without closing the throat.

One technique for curbing the reflexive opening of the vocal cords while in the act of breathing is to commence singing just before the completion of the inspiratory cycle. This will inhibit the normal shift of inspiratory muscular tension to expiratory tension. In effect, this technique will establish a balance between what would normally be an 'in' and 'out' movement of the breathing muscles. With the glottal space now closed, the abdominal wall will 'hold' position (without being 'held'), with the result that a genuine feeling of body poise will be established. Above all, the glottal space will remain closed *without being forced to close by the registration.*

Another device for closing the glottal space is to inspire comfortably, without raising the chest or tensing the shoulders, pausing for a fraction of a second before phonating. This practice is particularly useful for those involved with repertoire at an advanced level, where pure vocal technique is combined with musicianship and interpretation to evoke mood and atmosphere. Utilizing the breath in this manner, however, is not advisable unless the registration is in good order, and the resonance adjustment relatively free of constrictor tensions. No harm can come if this is attempted under less satisfactory conditions, but utilizing such a technique can be of real benefit only after an advanced stage of development has been reached.

It is of the utmost importance to note that the pause before singing stops the breath, thereby arresting respiration without closing the throat, as distinct from holding the breath, which would induce wrong tension. Stopping the breath momentarily before singing, when done correctly, should maintain the entire body in a poised attitude which encourages the possibility of natural movement. Technically, stopping the breath creates a balanced pressure between the thoracic muscles of inspiration and the abdominal muscles of expiration. Holding the breath makes natural movement impossible, inasmuch as it causes a stiffening of the expiratory muscles. Inability to fully release expiratory tension is the direct cause of the singer's failure to inspire freely.

With the glottal space closed by either of the techniques suggested above, the muscles drawing the vocal cords into tension are free to respond. With this freedom, provided the registers are well-balanced and coordinate effectively, the singer is able to devote his full concentration to interpretative matters. Because the cords approximate without interference, singing becomes quite effortless. If at the same time the larynx is well-positioned all basic technical problems will have been solved.

Neither of the breathing techniques discussed is of over-riding importance. Each should come quite naturally. Given this understanding, it is evident that training procedures can completely ignore all techniques given over to breath control and, largely, breathing as a direct vocal concern. The breath may possibly be considered the actuating force and, marginally, the sustainer of vocal tone. But it is equally clear that breath economy is due to an efficient coordinative process within the laryngeal pharynx, not a special technique of breathing. There are those who breathe incorrectly and sing extremely well, just as there are those who breathe properly and sing quite badly. No correlative factor between any technique of breathing and functional efficiency is anywhere evident, nor is such a proposition supported by scientific investigators. Good breathing habits help, but do not ensure, a good vocal technique.

To arrive at a more reasonable explanation of the importance of breathing to vocalization one must make a clear distinction between the organs of respiration and breath. Breath supplies oxygen to the system and eliminates carbon dioxide. Through combustion —the formation of compounds of body substances with oxygen— energy is created, the function of breathing being to increase the production of energy within the total organism. Organic life (movement) is made possible through the intake of oxygen, and it is the combustible energy within the organism itself which in all likelihood vitalizes the muscular activities which yield tone, not the pressure of the breath per se. Skill in singing, therefore, does not derive from any controlled system of breathing or 'breath support,' but from a healthy functional relationship (equilibrium) among the muscles involved in phonation. Understood in this way, the saying of the great baritone, Mattia Battistini, 'I take no more breath in singing than I do when smelling a flower' makes good sense. Breath pressure must be used, however, to sustain a vocal technique which lacks a precise muscular equilibrium.

Research conducted by a French scientist, Raoul Husson, brings the weight of scientific evidence to bear in support of what might otherwise remain an interesting hypothesis. Working with excised larynges and anesthetized dogs, he advanced the neurochronaxic theory, a theory which claims that the motor impulses from the central nervous system cause rhythmic contractions of the thyroarytenoid muscles producing the vibrations requisite to any given tone. Husson supports the contention that the vibrations of the vocal cords are to a large extent independent of breath pressure.

Assuming Husson to be correct, then the vocal folds must be thought of as self-vibrating, with the breath merely the element which forms and carries the sound. This conclusion seems to be consistent with observable data. Great singers, often expressing contradictory opinions about proper management of the breath, nevertheless seem always to have an unlimited supply regardless of the discrepancies in the techniques employed. This corroborates Husson's view and further inclines one to the belief that the vocal problem must be thought of as one which pertains to muscular coordination, not breath pressure.

A correct technique of breathing is, of course, desirable and represents an important phase of the attack. But to attempt to control function through control of the breath, as is commonly practiced, constitutes a manifest absurdity. Certainly breath is wasted and presents an obvious problem when the mechanism functions poorly, nor is there any question but what excessive energy is required to inject and sustain tonal vitality when the muscular coordination is at odds with itself. But shortness of breath and dissipation of energy are *effects* of a functional condition, not causes, and to confuse one with the other is to obscure the issue and confuse the student. The one legitimate concern with breathing is the neutralization of both inspiratory and expiratory tension so that the vocal cords, through the mechanics of registration, can approximate freely.

Phonation may now be seen to center on three distinct areas of function: breathing, which has an immediate effect upon the glottal position; registration, which determines the length, tension and contour of the vocal folds and which also influences the glottal position; and laryngeal suspension, a positioning process which is the qualitative factor in resonance. Since the vocal mechanism must be thought of as a totality, each of these aspects of technique is equal to the other. During the process of restructuring the technique, however, one will at one time or another assume greater importance. As a rule, registration is the first area to require attention, then the laryngeal suspension and breathing. Breathing itself falls into three categories: a technique for closing the glottis; another for assisting the 'letting go' process mentioned earlier with reference to registration; and, finally, breathing as it relates to emotion.

BREATH CONTROL

SINGING is so intimately bound up with the physical process of respiration, it is little wonder that the art of phonation touches upon the very essence of life itself. Registration, adjustments for resonance, rhythm, organic motility, emotion and kinetic sensitivity are all by-products of the respiratory process, and the singer's emotional, as well as vocal, life largely depends upon the kind of functional response the respiratory organs are capable of yielding.

The question naturally arising when attempting to correct a vocal problem, therefore, is where to start. Is it better to concentrate on a special technique of breathing? Or is it more advantageous to make corrections through the mechanics of registration and resonance? Opinion is still sharply divided on this issue. Historically, attitudes toward breathing have ranged from Cirillo's, 'My God! If you do not know how to breathe it is time you were buried,' to Pacchiarotti's, 'He who knows how to breathe and how to pronounce, knows how to sing.' Of the two, Pacchiarotti's assertion has gained wider acceptance and, with the passing of time, has become the basis upon which most modern methods are founded.

Pacchiarotti's statement, of course, meets no known standard of measurement. Many pronounce beautifully who could hardly be said to sing at all, while others breathe incorrectly and sing very well. Furthermore, those who breathe properly and pronounce well do not necessarily sing any better than those who do not. One tends in these matters to be easily taken in by such statements as Pacchiarotti's because of the artistic stature of the individual making the pronouncement. If, therefore, one cannot be made to literally believe Pacchiarotti, it might still be profitable to speculate on what he was *trying* to say, and how even this came to be distorted. By doing so, the question raised as to where instruction should begin will supply its own answer. If we are to chart a straighter course through troubled waters then, we must begin by questioning the significance of breathing itself, and especially its relationship to the artist as a person.

The artist pursues a goal in response to his inner vision. His thoughts and feelings must be channeled, and for this to be accomplished the respiratory organs (the organs of emotion) and the vocal organs (the mechanical process resulting in 'voice,' and especially muscular scaffolding which holds the larynx in poise and vitalizes the resonance) are made to assume the role of transmitting agent. The efficiency of this medium in terms of natural functioning will determine whether or not the singer's thoughts and feelings will be spontaneous or calculated. Inasmuch as it is a natural functioning which leads to spontaneity, it is this that demands attention. Without natural functioning, spontaneity, emotion, natural rhythm and kinetic sensitivity will be impaired. Release of function through release of respiratory tension, therefore, is crucial to the development of vocal skills.

As all spontaneous and natural functioning is an outgrowth of spontaneous and natural breathing, vocal training should start with the inculcation of healthy breathing habits. But phonation often contravenes the normal ebb and flow of natural breathing. In singing, allowance must be made for tonal duration, a factor which necessitates the maintenance of a narrowed glottal position for protracted periods of time. This narrowed position must remain constant regardless of the level of emotional involvement. Opposed to this, unchecked emotions cause the vocal bands to lose their tonicity, thus depriving them of their capacity to act as a vibrating agent. In two critical areas, therefore, spontaneous emotion often works against the singer's vocal interest, disturbing both reposeful breathing and the coordinative process which closes the glottal space. For the singer to totally give way to spontaneous emotion, especially when experiencing deeper layers of feeling, is to invite a serious disruption of the phonative process.

The problem here is that the performer must be able to express his innermost feelings without restraint, yet maintain his emotional equilibrium. To preserve this balance his emotions must be disciplined and to a degree controlled. 'Letting go' may be useful as psychotherapy and, indeed, is an essential feature of early vocal training; but it is a practice which must be employed with discretion. Art requires discipline; and there is a discipline controlling all artistic expression which, while self-regulating, must nevertheless be recognized and understood. The student is ready to emerge as an artist when he becomes aware of having made contact with the inner mechanics of self-regulation and discovers how to maintain its integrity in the face of highly charged emotional situations.

In striving for spontaneity the artist must therefore learn to strike a precarious balance between natural functioning and control over natural impulses. He must learn how to make others laugh and cry without laughing and crying himself; he must learn to be involved, yet aloof, to feel profoundly, yet stop short of being overwhelmed by his feelings. It is the 'cool head, but warm heart,' so often talked about. By 'feeling with his breathing,' the artist is able to regulate, control and maintain this precarious balance. Breathing techniques developed with this end in view, however, are concerned not with the mechanics of function, but with the mechanics of feeling.

A concept more acceptable to the vast majority of teachers down through the years is the distorted belief that control over function can best be achieved by controlling the breath, as to both the quantity to be released and the manner in which it is to be inspired and 'prepared.' The result has been that many who could otherwise have sung naturally (in the sense of utilizing a technique which operates in conformity with nature's laws), with freedom and spontaneity of expression, have been turned into vocal cripples. The failure to make a distinction between 'feeling with the breathing' and the institution of mechanical control over the vocal function by arbitrary techniques of breathing, remains to this day one of the major obstacles to free singing.

Maintaining one's emotional poise without introducing wrong tension demands the rejection of all systems given over to overt control of the breath. Most of us are rigid enough without being encouraged to hold a stiff posture, or to control the breath by holding it. Expansive movement must be encouraged, not discouraged. Yet if emotion is outward movement, one cannot expand *ad infinitum,* and certainly there is a point at which an easy equilibrium must be established in order to keep the emotions under control. It is the establishment of this equilibrium, better described as 'feeling with the breathing,' which the singer must master if he is to communicate without disrupting the mechanics of the phonative process.

The answer to the question raised earlier still is incomplete because control of the breath through control of the emotions is valid only when the motor response of the laryngeal musculature is efficient. Just as gasoline is wasted when a motor needs reconditioning so, too, breath is wasted when the laryngeal musculature is poorly coordinated. Thus, all valid control over breath expenditure is lost when the technique is faulty. Under these circumstances the singer should not be concerned about stabilizing his emotional involvement but with functional mechanics; his problem is not one of breath management, but one of awkward laryngeal muscles.

Short of the time when really advanced training begins, instruction in breathing should emphasize those aspects of technique which encourage naturalness of posture. There should be no raising of the chest or tensing of the shoulders, no pulling in or pushing out of the abdominal wall, no direct effort to expand the rib cage, and no indulgence in the often burdensome chore of breathing too deeply. The amount of breath to be used, the manner in which it is inspired, and the way it is utilized as an energic force will in the end be determined by the efficiency of the motor response within the laryngeal pharynx, by the precision with which the laryngeal muscles engaged in phonation position themselves. When this process is carried out without violating the healthy movement potential of the respiratory system, nature herself will dictate the manner in which the breath should be fed into the mechanism. A correct technique of breathing *follows* nature, rather than being made to act upon it.

There is, of course, a correct and an incorrect technique of breathing and every student must be so instructed. But breathing options are limited and the subject can, in theory and practice, be grasped without difficulty in a lesson or two.* To belabor the sub-

---

*As with all such propositions, this is true only insofar as the conditions are right. Psychological tensions stiffen the body and arrest free, natural movement. The world is full of shallow breathers, those who simply cannot inspire freely because of physical disabilities which are the reflection of deep rooted psychic tensions. From the standpoint of the teacher's responsibility this problem is relieved, not by stressing breathing techniques, which further aggravate the problem, but through the mechanics of registration. Breathing techniques will relieve psychic tensions it is true, but this responsibility falls on the qualified psychiatrist, not the voice teacher.

ject is to avoid more fundamental issues and encourage attitudes which increase rather than decrease psychic and physical tenseness. If one were to add a postscript to Pacchiarotti's statement it would have to be, 'He who arbitrarily controls his breathing often seems to want for breath.'*

In terms of function, all systems based upon direct control of the breathing apparatus are restrictive. They encourage throatiness and engender self-conscious attitudes which stiffen the body and inhibit natural movement. Total identification comes from within, and breath control, together with all outer imposed disciplines, must be discarded if the vocal function is to be free.

Why has Pacchiarotti's viewpoint on breathing persisted? Probably, it is due to the influence of the artist who, career over, decides to teach. Those falling into this category have frequently been blessed with 'natural' voices, voices which without formal training functioned extremely well. As a result, fundamentals were glossed over during their student days while attention was centered on matters pertaining to interpretation—style, text, emotion and tone 'color.' Consequently, registration is a natural endowment such an artist has taken for granted without really understanding its mechanics, while his knowledge of resonance is limited to that which he 'feels.' As an artist, he accepts his voice (and quite properly) as an instrument of expression; as a teacher, he teaches that which he knows, and the artist knows that breathing as an interpretive aspect of singing is important. His business is communication, and he is keenly aware of an existing correspondence between breathing and emotion.

Having for so long 'breathed life' into that which he sings, it is not difficult to see why, when he has been asked to help others, the successful performer teaches breath management instead of functional mechanics; expressive breathing has been an intimate

---

*Douglas Stanley, *The Science of Voice,* New York: Carl Fischer, Inc., 1929, was the first to scientifically expose this fallacy. Studies completed by William E. Ross at The University of Indiana and others by the Electrical Research Products, Inc., and The Bell Telephone Labs., also prove beyond doubt that Pacchiarotti's postulate is baseless.

part of his artistic life. Furthermore, it is obvious that the majority of students have trouble with their breathing. We live in an anxiety-ridden world, and shallow breathers (a product of anxiety) are the rule rather than the exception. It is perfectly natural to conclude, therefore, that the student's technical faults derive from his breathing problem. Consequently, correction would seem to lie within the province of breath 'management.'

The technical problems commonly faced in practical vocal training, however, are far removed from the area of feeling within which the artist functions so well. Few students have naturally well-formed voices and their ability to 'feel' is usually limited because of throat constriction. The problems to which the teacher must constantly address himself are: throat constriction, shortness of tonal range, lack of resonance, and the student's inability to execute even reasonably long phrases without running short of breath.

Not one of the faults mentioned above is directly caused by faulty breathing; none is subject to correction through techniques given over to control of the breath. Each falls within the province of function and is due to a poor muscular coordination within the laryngeal pharynx. When technical difficulties arise which lie within the area of functional mechanics, it is irresponsible to deal with the problem by attempting to control the breath. Generally, speaking, it is far more advisable to defer work on breathing until basic fundamentals have been well worked out. Breath management becomes a legitimate issue during advanced training when the student is ready to 'feel with his breathing' for purposes of interpretation. A vital point to remember is this: it is a properly adjusted larynx which to a great extent trains and regulates the breathing.

The interior mechanism which gives rise to 'voice' is at one and the same time a respiratory system, a digestive tract and a vocal apparatus. Each of these is strongly influenced by emotion. We cannot eat or digest food properly when upset, and respiration is disturbed during emotional stress. This reaction pattern carries over into the vocal function, so that in training it is often difficult to judge whether or not the problems lie within the sphere of faulty muscular coordination, imprecise mental concepts or emotional tension. Usually there is considerable overlap, and working through a vocal problem is like finding the exit to a labyrinth. Of the three, it is emotional attitudes which are most difficult to reconcile. Above all other factors, it is this which makes training the voice so precarious a proposition.

On the basis of the preceding discussion, it is evident that tonal beauty depends upon three things: sharpness of concepts as they relate to musical tone, precision of response on the part of the muscle groups involved in phonation, and psychological attitudes. Each of these plays an important role, and those who succeed in 'putting it all together' will be those who mature vocally and become artists. The principles upon which functional vocal training is founded are essential to vocal maturation. The respiratory organs, the barometer of the emotions, are the heart of that process.

CHAPTER XII

THE VIBRATO

$\mathbf{N}$OWHERE is the presence of inner rhythmic movement more apparent than in the oscillations normal to all musical tone. Tonal oscillations may be of various kinds: tremulous, wobbly, sporadic, or perfectly regular. Regular (rhythmic) oscillations are known as a vibrato, and the vibrato is one of the primary manifestations of a healthy vocal technique. Few singers use their voices correctly and, consequently, a true vibrato is rare.

A vibrato is readily distinguishable through its physical features —an amplitude which increases and decreases in direct proportion to the rise and fall of intensity, coupled with a periodicity which remains constant. Other tonal movements such as the tremolo and the wobble behave differently. With less desirable tonal movements, it will be found that the amplitude has little relationship to intensity, while the periodicity is disturbingly irregular. A useful rule of thumb in estimating the character of tonal pulses is to determine whether or not the fluctuations are *noticeable*. In a true vibrato, one is unaware of oscillating movements;

114

pitch appears to be centered, and the tone alive, vibrant, and beautiful.

An important feature of the vibrato is that it permits the voice to move rhythmically through the musical phrase; it establishes the voice as a legato instrument. When tonal oscillations are rhythmic, there is bound to be a moment in time when it is logical to move. This disposition to move does not necessarily occur in terms of the singer's sense of musical discipline, but within his organic logic. Such movements may not always coincide with the time values set by the composer, but they will be, nevertheless, *rhythmically* correct. Historically, many singers with but the most prosaic musicality have proved effective and phrased beautifully simply because their voices moved in response to a natural, free organic rhythm.

Above and beyond these important considerations, the vibrato is the reflector of the emotions, in speech as well as in song. The voice will tremble with rage, bubble with laughter, sound heavy with fatigue and despair, grow unsteady when depicting age, and, in general, reflect every emotion experienced by the singer. The vibrato indicates a healthy functioning vocal technique and is a sensitive barometer of the emotions. Technically, its appearance is due to a precisely balanced registration combined with an open-throated resonance adjustment. Artistically, it is an important and essential element in the development of musicianship and interpretation.

CHAPTER XIII

INTERPRETATION

THE inescapable truth concerning interpretation is that none of its mechanical aspects (correct tempi, sensitive phrasing, accuracy of intonation, good tone quality, correct diction, and knowledge of tradition) necessarily ensure an effective performance. Not even a magnetic personality is enough, although it helps overcome many shortcomings. As is also true with the mechanics of good manners, just being correct is not enough. Certainly the essence of a musical experience must lie elsewhere.

The substance of an effective performance is rhythm. Rhythm is inseparable from tempo (movement) and is instrumental in tracing the design of a musical phrase. It is also a factor in tone quality, since the vibrato oscillates in rhythmic patterns. Rhythm, synonymous with movement, is also associated with emotional expression. Thus, tempo, phrasing, tone quality and emotion may be said to possess a rhythmic essence from which the character of each is derived and without which vocalization would be empty and meaningless.

116

Rhythm forms an important link between technique and interpretation. Through rhythm contact is made with natural reflexes related to the production of tone. We are not referring to the kind of rhythm associated with 'keeping time,' or metric time, but to organic rhythm and the free movement of involuntary muscles, specifically, the laryngeal musculature and its auxiliaries. Organic rhythm encourages natural movement and is strongly instrumental in correcting technical faults. Another important feature of rhythm associated with natural movement is that the vocal mechanism becomes self-articulatory, indicating through an inner impetus the manner in which energy is to be expended. It is due to rhythmic identification of this description that the vocal organs and their functional needs become 'known' to the singer, i.e., understood as a kinetic experience. Before interpretation becomes a matter for serious concern, therefore, the ability of the vocal organs to respond freely to a rhythmic impetus must first be established.

There are three ways to promote organic rhythm and gain an understanding of natural movement. First, the singer must inspire evenly in the same tempo as the music. This should help him 'get with' the rhythm of each phrase before phonation begins and, by 'feeling with his breathing,' simultaneously gain contact with the natural muscular movements necessary to the production of vocal tone and the emotional properties of his musical material. The result will be that the phonative act and the feelings aroused by healthy organic movement will open the way to an easy identification with the words and music being sung.

The second approach is through an awareness of the tonal pulse contained within the vibrato. Because of the intrinsically rhythmic nature of the vibrato one is enabled to get the 'feel' of the tonal movement and, as with a well-executed golf swing, develop a concept of energy use which involves strength without forcing. The third approach utilizes those principles governing the mechanics of registration. These, when properly employed, improve the physical condition of the vocal organs and help restore lost motility. Taken together, the procedures here advocated will stimulate the rhythmic movement of involuntary muscles. They will also reveal the condition of the functioning mechanism and indicate the logical path to be followed for its continued development.

It should now be evident that interpretive skills rely heavily on rhythmic sensitivity and economy of movement. Ease of execution, beautiful tone quality, the ability to sustain long phrases, mechanical flexibility, durability, and a natural vibrato are all expressions of this economy. When the vocal muscles are poorly coordinated, or restricted in their movement because of psychic tensions, the inevitable result will be a general functional deficiency in all of these areas. Deficiencies which place a limitation on the singer's ability to execute also limit tasteful and imaginative interpretations.

'Getting with' the elan of a musical phrase or exercise, of course, encourages natural movement and operates as a powerful force in the correction of vocal errors. Obviously, the freedom of involuntary muscular movements depends upon the condition of the functioning mechanism and upon the effectiveness of the coordinative process. Limited technical resources offer limited interpretive options. One cannot phrase beautifully, pronounce pure vowels, 'shade' the voice, articulate with complete freedom, or, in general, possess a manageable instrument if the registers are 'mixed,' if throat constriction is present, or if the larynx is poorly suspended.

To improve function and bring the vocal system into equilibrium the procedures employed must utilize the principles governing registration and adjustment for resonance. Until such time as the technique has become stabilized creative interpretation expressed in acceptable vocal terms is impossible. At every step along the way, however, a conscious attempt must be made to infuse each exercise necessary to the retraining process with a rhythmic elan which encourages natural response patterns. In this way conscious controls can be relinquished and contact made with both spontaneous movement and spontaneous feeling.

The singer, therefore, in his formative years, must be treated like the young instrumentalist. Each must achieve considerable technical facility before sophisticated interpretations become a matter of serious concern. With the singer, the problem is somewhat more complicated. He is learning to 'build' and retrain his instrument, i. e., restructure his technique by changing the co-ordinative process which positions both the vocal cords and the larynx. To think in terms of pure aesthetics at such a time serves no practical purpose. Good musicianship serves to sustain and even improve the technique when the voice is already well formed, but it does virtually nothing for the singer who has vocal problems.

Several advantages are to be gained by stressing technique: 1) the discerning listener will discover a correspondence between stimulus and response and gain an insight into functional mechanics, 2) the freed mechanism will of itself indicate the path to be taken for its continued growth, and 3) the singer will have at his disposal greater technical command over his instrument; he will be able to refine his phrasing, 'color' the vowels, and phonate without having to 'produce' his voice or 'make' resonance. In short, he will have conscious knowledge of the tools at his disposal for the creation of legitimate musical and vocal effects.

The art of singing and the core of a moving interpretation may consequently be found to combine the mechanical aspects of music making with the kinetic movements to which they legitimately correspond. When these factors are balanced with intelligence and imagination, musical performance becomes transformed into art. To help bring the student to the point where he is able to identify with the expressive movements initiated within the deepest recesses of his being is the ultimate challenge of vocal pedagogy. Emotion awakened through free organic and muscular movement, guided by intelligence, refined by sensitivity and taste, and directed with imagination and understanding comprise the essence of an effective interpretation. Free rhythmic articulation binds function, intelligence, emotion and musical material into an entity—and, as Frrangçon-Davies (1855-1918) put it so succinctly, 'The whole muscular system from head to feet will be in the wise man's singing, and the whole man will be in the tone.'

There is, of course, a direct contradiction between the two points made with reference to natural movement and the physical condition of the vocal organs; for, if natural rhythmic movement relies upon spontaneous and well coordinated muscular reactions, it would seem obvious that a poorly coordinated mechanism would abort any effort made to utilize a rhythmic elan to improve the coordinative process. It is quite true, natural movement *is* stifled by poor muscular coordination, but the fact remains that a continuous effort must be made to work each scale pattern or exercise as rhythmically as possible. Natural rhythm is an elemental life process continually struggling for self expression. Both teacher and pupil must take advantage of this tendency and use it, in conjunction with registration, (which involves involuntary muscular adjustments and can be made to transcend both habitual response patterns and preconcepts) to work toward a continued improvement in the movement habits of those laryngeal muscles which position the vocal organs during phonation.

The need to reestablish the natural rhythmic potential of the vocal mechanism is self-evident. It is likewise evident that all of the physical skills related to tone which result in good phrasing, a pure legato, clean articulation, the ability to swell and diminish, flexibility, and an ability to 'color' the vowels are dependent upon a vocal technique operating in complete agreement with nature's laws. To believe, as many do, that technique can be improved through proper pronunciation of the text is patently false. It is, also, incorrect to believe that interpretation is a word oriented exercise. A correct pronunciation keeps technical matters in good order and, when the technique is sufficiently well advanced, will indeed improve the functional condition of the vocal organs to a degree. Correct diction, however, will neither correct serious vocal faults, nor will it infuse the interpretation with those properties which lend it the highest artistic values, namely, the ability to express thoughts and feelings at a level of communication which transcends word meanings.

At the heart of every language used in song and operatic literature lies the vowel form; and the vowel form is synonymous with the tonal form. If the tone is poorly produced, the vowel will be poorly formed and impure. From the standpoint of techique, impure vowels deprive the voice of its beauty, its expressive capacity and spontaneous feeling as well. Beautiful, expressive language comes from a well formed voice, but a well formed voice does not come from either good pronunciation or beautiful language. The building of interpretive skills, therefore, must be worked through techniques related to function and not, as is so often the case, by means of poetic imagery having little or nothing to do with the enhancement or preservation of a healthy vocal technique.

In the final analysis, the ability to unleash one's creative imagination depends upon that individual's ability to express himself through natural rhythmic movement. It is for this reason that each of the elements necessary to artistic singing must be considered an extension of a rhythmic impetus which binds technique, language, imagination, the text, and the musical structure into an entity. Success in this will strike a responsive cord in both listener and performer far more penetrating than would any of the contributing elements be able to offer on its own. From the standpoint of the performer as a person and an artist, a notable advantage will have been gained—self-searching will have been replaced by self-discovery.

Rossini, a great voice teacher as well as composer, revealed in his conversations with Richard Wagner a profound insight into the manner in which interpretative skills are to be developed. In his view, three definite steps were taken: 1) the building of the instrument, 2) technique, the use of the instrument, and 3) style, of which the ingredients are taste and feeling. Tosi shared the view common to the time when he advocated a similar sequence. He emphasized the need for pure vowels, after which articulation in the form of solfege was introduced. This procedure formed a solid basis of technique upon which the sublties of language could find expression. To hope to develop a technique where the registers are well balanced, the vowels pure, and the technique free through the use of language disciplines is to invite the pedagogic failures that have been too long with us. The techniques of singing subscribed to by the master teachers of the 17th, 18th and 19th centuries are as valid today as they were then. Whether the music be tonal or atonal a technique which reflects functional freedom will be able to meet every demand made upon it. The singer who has acquired such a technique will then be able to participate fully in the artistic experience. He will have the technical means to express his innermost thoughts and feelings and project them to the listener.

ARTICULATION

PROVIDED a secure technical groundwork has been laid, articulation should present no problem. Again, 18th and 19th century practice indicates the best course to be taken when structuring the technique, and the general admonishment of the time to, 'Let the student learn to pronounce the vowels purely, else he has failed to advance beyond the first lesson,' should still be taken seriously. In former times consonants were never introduced until the student had made 'some remarkable progress.' First concerns were logically centered on function. After a secure technique had been established, art and aesthetics become increasingly important. Because of the technical groundwork which enabled the student to form pure vowels, the problems now so commonly associated with articulation, were found to be either easily soluble or non-existent.

The key to free articulation lies with the development of a vocal technique in which the energy used is largely concentrated within the tone. A mistake frequently made when the words are not clearly distinguishable is to stress the articulation. A more sensible approach is to energize the tonal vibrations, avoiding in the process both tongue and jaw stiffness.

A basic exercise for the development of clean articulation is to establish a well formed tone on the tonic, using any primary vowel, but preferably 'ah.' Next, continuing to energize the vibrations contained within the vowel, immediately introduce the syllable 'la' for the balance of the eight tone scale. In this way, the articulation will be both clean and relaxed. Extending this principle, exercises can be made to include other vowels and consonants to ultimately embrace language in its more sophisticated forms.

When the enunciation is free of tenseness the singer's words will not only be clearly distinguishable, but economical in terms of energy expenditure. Because there is little conflict between tone and articulation neither process will interfere with the other. The error to be constantly avoided is the over-stressing of consonants.

There are three prerequisites to free articulation: 1) vowel purification through the mechanics of registration and a correct laryngeal suspension, 2) the use of solfege, which would incorporate consonants without disturbing the vibrations associated with resonance and the vowel, and 3) to finally introduce the subtleties of language. By following the procedure here advocated, tone need never be sacrificed for clean enunciation, nor clean enunciation for the tone. Indeed, when the technique is well-formed, each should serve to enhance the efficiency of the other.

Expressive language, poetic imagination and free articulation all depend upon a vocal technique which is functionally healthy. Training procedures, therefore, must be designed to free the voice and perfect the coordinative process. In short, proceed from the easy to the difficult.

Three basic themes have been treated in these pages: 1) the mechanical principles which govern function, 2) the effect of psychological factors on movement potential, and 3) the need to trust the instincts so that, together with reason and common sense, each is made to participate as equal partners in the vocal process. Dr. Arne, in his famous setting of 'PREACH NOT ME YOUR MUSTY RULES', knew the full meaning of the need to trust the instincts when he set the words:

'Preach not me your musty rules,
Ye drones that mold in idle cell.
The heart is wiser then the schools,
The senses always reason well.'

Muscular and psychological equilibrium and an ability to trust one's instincts are essential to the learning process. Without these all efforts to interpret will fall short of the mark.

APPENDIX I

STIMULATION OF INVOLUNTARY MUSCLES

Before natural body rhythms can be set into motion, the conditions must be right. Here the student must develop a new attitude toward learning. In effect, he must learn to prepare by not preparing. He must face the difficulty of 'getting out of his own way,' of 'letting go,' of 'allowing things to happen,' and of being willing to lose all control, control which is related to nonfreedom and an absence of spontaneity. Should he succeed in this, the natural movements which will spring into being should provide a means of access to the muscular processes operating below the threshold of consciousness; that is to say, the important muscular activities which are related to phonation.

When contact has been made with interior body rhythms, the vocal organs, provided the proper stimulus patterns have been selected, will of their own disposition seek to move in a manner more in keeping with the functional logic by which they are governed. In short, like a wound that heals itself, the organs of voice will correct themselves—by responding more freely, they will

124

adapt to the congenial climate to which they have been exposed. What the student must do is give in to an inner-directed impetus, and, by following and observing, learn the nature of vocal control.

Natural breathing offers the best example of what is meant by 'getting out of the way' so that one can learn how to assist spontaneous organic rhythms. Breathing is both voluntary and involuntary. By removing all disciplines affecting the way one breathes, the act of inspiration and expiration will proceed naturally on an involuntary basis. Therefore, by observing the natural rhythm of breathing, one is able to perceive the sensation of movement, and so learn the mechanics of the function.

The moment one becomes aware of the natural rhythm of involuntary breathing, there should be no great difficulty in learning how to assist that movement through volitional effort, and to breathe either shallowly or deeply without losing the natural rhythm. This is the only sure way of gaining contact with a purely natural movement. Not until an inner force indicates the direction in which movement should be encouraged can one possess insight into the nature of an organic function and be in a position to institute legitimate control.

All muscles which respond to the inner rhythmic impetus of the vocal organs are, of course, involuntary. By keeping volitionally controllable muscles passive through nonmovement, a perception of interior movement can be gained. Under these conditions, all movement will be completely involuntary. Thus the singer, by observing, can sense the order, the logic, the impetus, and the laws of the vocal function. By proceeding in this manner, it is possible for him to maintain the integrity of his singing, both technically and interpretatively, because he has come to understand functional needs.

Awareness of inner movements and their natural rhythm is achieved by combining the rhythm of natural breathing with the movement of the musical phrase—its contour, intensity pattern, and vowel. At the onset of phonation, the posture of the body should reflect a condition of poised readiness, very much like that of a good dancer who is *about* to move. Then, without raising the chest or tensing the shoulder muscles, sufficient breath should be inspired to answer the needs of the musical phrase. With all volitionally controllable muscles maintained in a state of passivity, the rib cage will naturally expand. Upon sensing that contact has been made with the rhythm of the inspiratory movement, one must launch the phrase without disturbing the rhythmic impulse, *con slancio,* with a sense of continuing movement.

The next step to be taken is to devise an exercise pattern containing at least one variable. A simple major triad, to be sung on the vowel 'ah' at a comfortable level of volume, fills this requirement nicely. Having initiated the attack in the manner prescribed, the student's next point of concentration is the detail of the musical phrase—the pitches, the vowel, and the levels of intensity—and singing musically. Further, he must obliterate from his mind all concepts dealing with what he *thinks* his voice should sound like, or how he would *like* it to sound; he must be ready to 'do' without being conscious of the manner of 'doing'; he must 'get out of his own way' so as to permit involuntary movements to take over, to let nature operate on her own terms.

With voluntary muscles now passive, the variable element in the triad (pitch) becomes the main point of interest. When vocalizing, the student must make certain to concentrate on moving from pitch to pitch *mentally,* prohibiting all external movement. This is not easy, and the teacher must take great care to ensure that no stiffness is permitted to creep in. If the exercise is sung correctly (with a proper register balance and as pure a vowel as the singer can manage), the involuntary muscles governing the functional response at the point of tonal inception will have been activated. Because peripheral tensions to a considerable extent will have been lessened, important changes will occur in the organic response. New sounds will appear, sound which will serve to alter the student's self-image and make him aware of the 'feel' of the functional elements at work. Under this regimen, contact will have been made with natural inner organic movement.

HISTORICAL
BACKGROUND
OF REGISTRATION

According to Manuel Garcia (1805-1906) a register is a series of homogeneous sounds produced by one mechanism, differing essentially from another series of equally homogeneous sounds produced by another mechanism. While this explanation of the vocal registers has been universally accepted, it is nevertheless imprecise and subject to misinterpretation, the word 'homogeneous' being especially troublesome. Ventriloquists make strange sounds which are often homogeneous, to cite an extreme example, but even the normal voice is capable of making numerous types of sounds which could answer the same description. At best, trying to establish mechanical principles by describing the tone qualities to which they are related is a hazardous undertaking.

A brief summary of the nomenclature adopted by the greatest teachers of the Golden Age of Singing will indicate some of the difficulties encountered when applying Garcia's definition. Mancini (1716-1800) noted that, 'the voice ordinarily divides itself into two registers' (22). He and Manfridini (1737-1799) shared the same view and used the terms falsetto and head voice interchange-ably. A famous predecessor, Tosi (1647-1727), likewise recog-nized two divisions, but referred to the upper as 'the falsetto or feigned voice,' (12). Isaac Nathan (1791-1864), a direct descend-ant of the great Porpora, is the only writer to have clearly defined the 'feigned' voice, but he placed it within an entirely different context. He says, 'where the throat appears the chief organism connected with the production of sound, it is called a throat voice, termed in Italian, falsetto: and . . . where the process of breath-ing seems more than usually connected with the nostrils, and the sound is accordingly modulated by their influence, it is termed a head voice, in Italian, "voce di testa." ' He further states, 'I am aware that the falsetto is considered a feigned voice—but the quality of the sound to which I allude is not that which is pro-duced in the throat, and already distinguished under the name falsetto; nor is it the voce di testa' (4).

Another noted teacher, Tenducci (1737-?), seems to have adopted a position closer to that of Mancini, since he advised his students to 'cultivate the voce di testa in what is called the falsetto' (23). Francesco Lamperti (1813-1892) ignored the fal-setto but did recognize two registers in the male voice, the chest and mixed. The female voice he thought to be comprised of three —the chest, mixed, and head (24). Garcia held that the middle voice range and falsetto of the female voice were one and the same mechanism—assigning the head voice to the upper tonal range. However, like Lamperti, he seems to have found no direct parallel between the male and female voice; as he said, 'In men's voices, as in women's, the three registers coexist, but the chest predominates, the other two being but a remnant of the boy's voice (8).

To further obscure the issue, various aspects of registration were also described as mezzo falso, voix mixte, the voce di gola, the voce di piena, the flute voice, and the thick, thin and small registers—the latter grouping sometimes being subdivided into 'lower thick and lower thin,' 'upper thick and upper thin,' and 'small.' Herbert Witherspoon (1873-1935) charted an entirely different course when he stated categorically that, 'There is but one register of the human voice, and only one, but there are three distinct qualities, the chest quality, the mouth quality, the head quality, and these are simply due to resonation in the three districts mentioned (13).*

The above consensus demonstrates four things: 1) that 'breaks' and 'lifts' are a common vocal phenomenon, 2) that a rather free-wheeling terminology distorts what in most cases could have been a set of clearly understood propositions, 3) that homogeneous qualities are aural phenomena not easily definable in concrete terms, often being merely subjective evaluations growing out of personal experience, and 4) that the issue remains obscure because the formulations neglect to mention the functional arrangements which give rise to, and are responsible for, a given series of homogeneous sounds.

Garcia's definition is therefore somewhat misleading. The mechanical features of the 'mechanisms' referred to are never stated and the entire thrust of his meaning centers on the word 'homogeneous.' This has led to a serious misconception in contemporary pedagogic thinking, an error based on the falacious conclusion arrived at by Witherspoon. According to Witherspoon a register is simply a quality. But, were his concept of 'mouth quality' to be taken seriously, what functional mechanics could be said to be involved? None, of course!

The unfortunate aspect of the terminology employed by those who have adopted Witherspoon's reasoning is that all reference to

---

*Witherspoon's viewpoint reflects the belief and practice of the bulk of contemporary teachers. Such views, as will be shown, completely discard practical mechanical principles, substituting instead what Garcia described as 'mere appearances.' If one were to be searching for any single factor which could account for the disappearance of the art of Bel Canto singing the quest would end here. Mouth, head and chest resonance are virtually nonexistent, nor does such a concept take into account the quality of the vibratory impulses set in motion by the vibrating cords. Garcia was also correct when he said, 'all control over the tone is lost once the cords become vibratile.' The quality of the vibrations emanating from the cords is determined by the efficiency of the vibrating member which, in turn, is influenced by an intricate muscular process involving the entire respiratory tract.

the *source* of tonal vibrations is ignored while the *by-products* of those vibrations are held to be their cause. No vocal organs exist in the head or chest cavities. Consequently, no mechanical action can take place there. What each mechanical arrangement *awakens,* however, is a specific symptom of vibration, originating within the larynx, which *appears* to be located either in the head or in the chest, depending upon the type of coordinative process currently operative. This, being so, the basic problem in voice training is learning how to gain access to the mechanism, to discover how the vocal organs can be stimulated into predictable types of response. If one desires a particular kind of homogeneous sound, then one must be familiar with the specific mechanical formula which will yield that tone quality.

In passing, it may be useful to note that there is an abundance of scientific evidence to discredit the validity of both mouth and head resonance. William Vennard *(Singing: The Mechanism and the Technic)* quotes a passage from a doctoral dissertation, unpublished, by Charles Frederick Lindsley, University of Southern California, 1932, which expresses without frills the essence of scientific consensus:

> If the conventional theories concerning head resonance and the function of the sinuses are true, it would be logical to expect falsetto tones to incite the greatest response in the small resonators. The tenor who served as a subject was able to sing and sustain beautiful falsetto tones. The actual amount of vibration measurable at the point of the sinus was very small . . . and the amount of chest vibration was correspondingly large . . . The maximum intensity of vibration was recorded at the point of the larynx and trachea . . . (this) relates to the general position derived from this study; namely, that voice quality differences are conditioned primarily by the structure of the vocal bands (25).

APPENDIX III

FUNCTIONAL STUDIES

To facilitate the discovery of functional laws, it is necessary to project a wide variety of stimulus patterns. In this way one can discover similarities and dissimilarities within the dynamics of the process, namely, stimulus, organic response, and tonal texture. A procedure of this kind raises important questions. Is the response always the same? Are there textural differences which can be equated with a particular type of stimulus? If so, what kind of relationship can be discovered?

Analyzing reflex responses assumes that a better than average vocal technique is being studied. Poor reflexive responses obscure nature's laws, and all attempts to discover functional truths will fail if conclusions are arrived at on the basis of inadequate material. Only free voices, expressing a consonance with nature, will reveal the mechanical principles upon which a correct vocal technique is founded.

To begin, suppose the student, a soprano, has been instructed to sing a descending C major scale at a comfortable level of intensity on the vowel 'ah,' with the further request to preserve at all costs (even at the risk of sacrificing tonal vitality) the textural properties established on the topmost tone. If this instruction is carried out faithfully, only one course will be left open—she must gradually decrease the amount of pressure applied, and consequently, the intensity.

Carrying this experiment further, it will be discovered that exactly the same reaction occurs, under the same set of conditions, while singing other vowels. Of added interest is the fact that the noticeable point of difficulty always seems to be located in the vicinity of F, immediately above middle C. Now a question arises. Why do the lower tones of the scale, provided the textural properties of the upper tones are maintained throughout, grow progressively weaker?

Before answering, let us revise the scale pattern and investigate other alternatives. Of particular interest is the pitch area below middle C. Using a single tone on the vowel 'ah' and commencing at B flat, or perhaps A, the student is now requested to raise the intensity and sing at a comfortable forte. Now what happens? The entire structure of the preceding tonal texture will automatically and reflexively undergo a radical change! Sweetness will have given way to a rugged, almost masculine sound, a quality which can be recognized as the chest register.

Having made the discovery that within certain tonal areas the reflex response of the vocal organs is predictable, and having further discovered that an equation exists between response and stimulus, we may now be said to have made contact with a natural functional activity. At no point in the instruction was the student asked to 'produce' a specific kind of sound; the sound produced itself. It emerged as a logical, natural reaction to an environment. This is the essence of functional training. It leads to tonal naturalness, to spontaneity, and to self-awareness.

Suppose, now, we try to discover whether or not the student is able to connect these two characteristically different sounds she has been made aware of. This will, of course, necessitate the use of a larger musical figure, so an arpeggio covering a range of one octave and a fifth will be useful. The vowel to be used is 'ah,' the starting note A, below middle C, the intensity forte.

In attempting this figure, the student soon finds that a smooth connection is impossible and that a disruption of the tonal flow occurs between the first and second notes. Thus, we learn that there is a 'break' in the voice. As the student was requested to sing smoothly, it again becomes clear that the break is also reflex to a specific arrangement within the stimulus pattern. What transpired is this: the chest register responded willingly on the tonic because the pitch-intensity pattern prompted its emergence. As the voice moved upward, however, the third above the tonic proved unmanageable, a situation to which the vocal organs readily accommodated by changing registers. Again the conclusion is unavoidable—that a change in the pitch-intensity pattern is naturally accompanied by a corresponding change in the registration.

Examining the cause of the break will reveal that the crossing of the two registers occurs in the upper portion of the tonal range of the chest register where the intensity is always high, and in the lower portion of the head register where the intensity is quite low. This fact is of great importance to the training program, because it enables the teacher to manipulate the *interior processes* of the mechanism and revitalize its function. If there were no such thing as a register response to correlative patterns of pitch and intensity, very little could be accomplished toward promoting an improvement in the functional condition of the vocal organs.

Other interesting possibilities soon suggest themselves. If the student is instructed to execute the identical musical figure, with the single exception that it be sung at a strong mezzo piano, or a slack mezzo forte, yet another type of involuntary response will take place. As a reaction to this type of change within the stimulus pattern, the vocal organs will display a reflex tendency *to combine the two textures* recognized as belonging to the chest and head register, first minimizing, then eliminating the break. Keeping the textural properties of the registers in mind, it is immediately evident that, with the break between the registers bridged over, a third tonal texture has made its appearance. Again, this texture was not sought after, but appeared reflexively in response to the changed stimulus pattern. This condition might advantageously be called a coordinated registration, combining as it does the activity of *both* registers, which now operate as a functional entity.

In establishing the concept of registration as a functional reflex, it develops that three separate sets of conditions can be induced by rearranging the stimulus patterns: 1) the falsetto, or head register, 2) the uncoordinated chest register, and 3) a combined, or co-ordinated registration. Shortly, a fourth possible arrangement will be brought under discussion, a mixed registration.

We have now seen that under specific conditions vocal organs habitually respond in a manner both consistent and predictable. We have also discovered that the responses are reflex to a specific type of stimulus, the stimulus itself being comprised of pitch, intensity, and the vowel. Some of these arrangements tended to create tonal textures which divided the mechanism into two separate units, while others obliterated the inner mechanics and unified the function.

So we have discovered a correspondence between a given pitch-intensity pattern and the texture of tone yielded. Therefore, the question raised earlier as to why both the tonal texture and the intensity soften with the descent of the C major scale can be answered. In our first experiment with a stimulus pattern, the head voice was encouraged to maintain its characteristic texture. If the singer had *failed* to decrease the intensity with the descent of the scale, this would have been impossible. Regardless of any effort made to avoid a textural change, the higher intensity level would automatically engage some element of chest register participation. Only by singing more softly was it possible to maintain the head register balance. In physical terms, the effect of this disengagement was to fragment the mechanism. Consequently, the contour of a pure head register, obscured in a combined registration, was revealed.

From the standpoint of practical application, the predictable response of the vocal organs to the musical idea contained within the pitch, intensity, and vowel pattern presents many opportunities for assisting a more efficient functional response. We have just seen how the head register can be disengaged from its unitary function with the chest register, indicating that the teacher can arbitrarily balance the mechanism in a variety of ways. There is a second alternative. Should a stimulus pattern be introduced that would serve to isolate the chest register from contact with the head voice—for example, singing forte on a single tone in the lowest possible tonal range—the division of the registers, whenever such division is necessary, can be speeded. In this manner, two normally integral parts of the mechanism can be made to work independently.

The conclusion to be reached from these observations points up the real significance of voice-building. For if it is true that the mechanism is susceptible to disengagement of its parts, it then follows that the entire coordinative process is equally susceptible to reconditioning. That is to say, when necessary, it can be taken apart, tidied up, and put back together again in what should be a healthier functional order.

Ideally, there is but one mechanism, and unless all of the parts operate as a harmonious functional unit, there will be a serious loss of power, range, flexibility, and evenness of scale. However, a complete integration of the parts is not usually an immediate aim of functional instruction. Deficient areas of development must be corrected and brought up to strength before unification is feasible. Premature unification "builds in" limitations. The important point is that the means are now at hand for reconstructing a poor vocal technique.

Returning again to the subject of nature's laws, it should be clear that we have observed some of these laws in operation. None of the physiological, anatomical, or acoustic phenomena may as yet be understood. Nevertheless, from a pragmatic standpoint, the evidence clearly indicates that these laws have been operative. Contact with functional law is essential to a durable technique, and the means here described open the way for the establishment of that contact.

APPENDIX IV

A 'MIXED' REGISTRATION

In a mixed registration, the two registers, instead of working as a harmonious, cooperative entity, conflict with each other. A fairly accurate picture is provided by imagining two people of unmatched stride lengths walking side by side. Rather than moving rhythmically, the couple constantly collide because their steps are out of phase. Thus, natural movement is impeded and walking together not only becomes difficult, but unpleasant. In principle, this is exactly what happens in a mixed registration. The chest register, which when healthy is robust and powerful and should at the extreme go no higher than E, above middle C, becomes thinned out by being driven too high and made to intrude into a tonal area fully an octave higher than it ought to go. The head voice also presents a problem, because its pattern of response will have been forced out of character by the more aggressive quality of the chest register. Muscular activities which should work together harmoniously become mutual irritants.

So it may be seen that a mixed registration is also a muscular

136

reflex to an outer stimulus of pitch and intensity, but a badly coordinated arrangement. The chest register operates far too high
into the pitch range at an intensity far too low, while the head
register is disrupted by this intrusion and becomes incapable of
responding in a way natural to its own functional interest. A
mixed registration will always seriously impair the natural beauty
of the voice, with a consequent loss of range, power, and resonance.

A mixed registration is common to all voice types and seems to
receive encouragement from two major sources, training and cul-
ture. In outlining possible cures, it is necessary to discuss the male
and the female voice separately; it must be clear, however, that
there is absolutely no functional difference between them, the sole
difference being one of tonal range, women singing an octave
higher than men.

Our cultural attitude decrees, long before formal voice training,
that women speak in the head voice, that this is more feminine.
As a result, the chest register is left unused and, being unanchored,
is free to drift into a tonal area far too high, in the region of C,
above middle C, to the fourth above. This causes the voice to become weak in the lower range, overly strong in the upper middle,
and somewhat short-ranged and 'spread' on top. As the chest
register cannot tolerate reduced levels of volume, even within its
legitimate tonal range, it becomes badly thinned out when forced
higher and constricts the throat.

Correcting a mixture of this kind is difficult. The chest register
cannot be two places at once. If it is active in the upper middle
range, it is not able to respond in the tonal area to which it rightfully belongs. For this reason, it is often unwise to attempt to
establish contact with the chest register until the mixture is corrected. The theory behind this practice is obvious: if there are two
parts to the whole, by isolating and purifying one part, the other
automatically disengages and becomes pure. Thus, before any
serious attempt is made to use the chest register, the upper mechanism must be isolated.

Inasmuch as a mixed registration tends to fatten the upper
middle voice range at the expense of the outer parts, this condition

must be alleviated by establishing the pure falsetto. As its range lies between B, below middle C, and the octave above (which is true regardless of the singer's sex or voice type), exercises comprised of a single tone, major thirds, or a simple triad must be used. Since the pure falsetto is breathy, tonal clarity should be discouraged. The most favorable vowel to be employed is 'oo,' with the intensity on the lower tones held to a low level. At the same time, the upper fourth of the octave should be quite firm and, with men's voices, extremely full. Exercises of this kind must not be overworked and, once the falsetto has been established (which means that chest register interference has been eliminated), other scale patterns must be used.

Subsequent exercises for working the chest register out of the middle voice range where it does not belong must utilize the principles governing registration in more sophisticated combinations. One such approach is the octave interval with a descending arpeggio. The first note, usually E or F, must be sung firmly with good depth and solidity so that the tonal weight is anchored. Moving from the lower to the upper tone, a true legato must be preserved, but at the same time the weight must be left on the bottom note, as the upper octave is taken lightly at a firm mezzo piano. This practice should introduce a softer tonal texture, the appearance of which will indicate that the registers have begun to separate. It is important in descending the arpeggio that the tonal weight which was subtracted while moving upward is added again, thus rebalancing the mechanism toward the chest register in the lower tonal range. The most favorable vowel for this exercise is 'ah,' the exercise itself moving in descending patterns from E or F, if possible, to the octave below.

Since the voice, like an elastic band, can be weakened in the middle by being stretched in both outer directions, extension of the tonal range is also imperative. A useful preliminary exercise is to start on the upper tonic and move to the third above, then descend on an arpeggio of one octave and a third. In this way, the upper register will be pulled away from the improper mixture in the upper middle range—under which circumstance the head voice should take over the task for which it is so well suited. The 'ah' and the 'ee' vowels are helpful in this, and the exercise must be sung at full intensity. Care must always be taken in working these exercises to preserve the purity of the vowel and to avoid 'spreading.'

Another scale pattern which helps extract some of the tonal weight from the upper middle range is the double octave arpeggio. This exercise should commence on the lower G and progress step-wise as far as is practical. The intensity level throughout must remain at a firm mezzo piano, the upper tones not being permitted to burgeon out. If worked successfully, considerable stress will have been placed on the head voice, with chest register participation minimized. The voice should now be more buoyant and less 'grabby' in the upper area and, if so, the chest register should be ready to reappear where it rightfully belongs—in the lower tonal range.

At this point, single tones should be employed to test the articulation of the chest register. Should it respond, a whole world of possibilities opens up. Soon the resonance adjustment can be directly worked on to good effect. After the chest register has been consolidated, octave jumps are helpful, the low tone being started in a strong chest register, the upper note taken in the head voice. The purpose here is to take advantage of the fact that the chest register will have opened the throat. This being so, the skip into the octave above, provided the singer has not moved, should accommodate the upper register within the identical resonance adjustment formed by the chest register. If these exercises have been correctly executed, the singer will have sensed a new adjustment for the upper tone, an adjustment which will be freer and more open-throated. Again, it must be stressed that throughout all these exercises the instruction to not move is important. This is particularly true of the octave jump, as the purpose of this exercise is to change the registration (a reflex response), but not the resonance adjustment.

If the octave jump is well executed, both function and concept immediately become more viable. With the release of wrong muscular tensions, the vocal organs themselves, articulating their own

functional laws, tend to dictate the character of subsequent instruction. Obviously, new situations demand new stimulus patterns,
and the new requirements of the mechanism often call for remedies
diametrically opposed to those which had worked so well at an
earlier stage of development.

Other exercises for the release of interfering tensions are the
trill, the staccato, and rapid scales. The staccato is especially helpful in creating an awareness of laryngeal activity, for unless the
laryngeal suspension resists the energy expended, it is impossible
to execute this musical effect. When the larynx does hold position,
the student is able to feel what it is like to have the throat actively
open. (Garcia called this action the *coup de glotte,* stroke of the
glottis, which, because of its being so widely misinterpreted, is a
practice now totally discredited).

If the staccato is well executed, the concept of laryngeal activity
can easily be carried over into the legato phrase. To preserve the
connection between the legato and the staccato, each can be alter-
nated, the arpeggio first being sung staccato, the second time legato.
The easiest way to do this is to sustain the top tone the second
time around so that both the legato and the staccato continue to
share an identical position of resonance. Rhythm is important to
a good staccato, and the feeling should be one of a pendulum
freely moving.

Some contact should now have been made with the singer's
instinct for oral expression, leading, in turn, to a sensual awareness
of functional needs. Rapid scale passages are important at this
time. If organic functions are recognized as being rational, the
vocal organs must be given every opportunity to respond in terms
of their innate logic. Rapid scale passages provide such an opportunity. Here the student must resist the impulse to control the
voice. Concentration must be directed toward naturalness of posture, toward following the design of the melodic figure, the vowel,
and the intensity pattern, and 'getting with' the rhythmic sweep of
the phrase, nothing else. Of paramount importance is the fact that
the rhythmic impetus must begin with the intake of breath, before
phonation, and that all of the notes of the scale are conceptualized

as a unit. Rhythmically, one moves *through* the tonic, *through* the upper octave, and then back to the tonic. Provided the psychological barriers have been successfully overcome, the vocal organs should have already begun to assume a position of open-throated resonance.

How to utilize the exercises suggested above is, of course, a matter of judgment. They must be employed on a discretionary basis in varying combinations, and there is no format or order of procedure to be followed. Like good cooking, it is a little of this and a little of that, then seasoned to taste. It must be reemphasized, however, that it is the chest register alone which is capable of eliminating a throat constriction. It must also be stressed that, regardless of the pitch and intensity level, in a correct technique, the head register is always the dominant factor. Arranging the technique so that the nominally weaker mechanism becomes dominant is an apparent contradiction which has to be successfully resolved if the voice is to be free.

The problem with men's voices would appear to be far less severe and more easily corrected than would be the case with women. All male voices have access to a considerable amount of chest register, at least an octave and a third, and this provides a strong opening wedge for the release of constrictor tensions. In reality, however, the male voice simply presents different problems. Tenors offer an example of one basic difficulty, since their range straddles the register break. Consequently, unless they solve the problem of register transition successfully, they will either fail to acquire their high tones or constrict the throat. To a slightly lesser degree, this is a basic cause of constriction with basses and baritones.

Making a smooth register transition is difficult. At the moment of transfer, the chest register is operating in its upper tonal range, where the intensity is quite high. At the same time, the chest register must be coordinated with the head voice, which at the transition point is rather weak. This requires careful manipulation of the intensity, as well as the vowel. Errors of execution will immediately show up in the form of throat constriction. A rule of thumb is this: Enough chest register strength must be maintained at the transition point to keep the throat open, while the head register must be encouraged to take over as the dominant factor in the technique.

Other devices for opening the throat are the 'straight' tone and the vowel 'a' as in 'cat.' Each of these serves the same purpose, namely, to establish a sense of laryngeal resistance. For straight tones (tones with no oscillating movement), an arpeggio sung on the vowel 'ah' is ideal. By pushing the tone straight, contact will have been made with an open-throated position which, by being pressed gently outward, can be maintained throughout the duration of the phrase. When this exercise is executed correctly, the tone will change; it will commence to pulsate regardless of the steady pressure being applied.

An important aspect of this exercise is that the new pulse will bypass the singer's preconcept. As a result, he will not only discover how to energize the correct laryngeal action, but to hear new sounds in relation to his own personality. The 'a' vowel achieves somewhat the same result and basically serves a similar purpose. One must be certain in using this vowel that the lips do not spread and that the easy resonance of the chest register is never lost. It is also important that the intensity of the upper notes of the scale is not permitted to exceed that of the tonic.

To list all of the variations now possible would be impractical. Exercises repeadted again and again become dull, so variety for the sake of variety is often desirable. With technical development, however, one exercise is indispensable—the double octave arpeggio. It can be effectively used at all levels of intensity, preferably on the vowels 'ah,' 'ee,' and 'oo,' and every effort must be made in working this exercise to preserve the legato connection. Double octave scales are virtually foolproof and contain within themselves a tendancy to rebalance the mechanism. An important benefit of this practice is that it will decrease the excessive tension in a mixed registration and permit the chest and head voices to shift into their rightful areas of operation. Theoretically, the double octave arpeggio should effectively combine the registers and, when the overall intensity is gradually increased through practice, pave the way for a beautifully executed *messa di voce*.

Exercises for opening the throat are virtually the same for men as for women, and those discussed can be used interchangeably. As a mixed registration is usually at the root of most technical difficulties, the first procedure is to realign the registration. With an improved registration and the throat relieved of its closing tension, the resonance adjustment commands greater attention. In attacking this problem, the functional response of the registers is pitted against the psychic, as well as physical, impediments barring the way. Nature herself offers an assist at this point, because after proper development the chest and head register mechanisms will balance themselves reflexly. But it must not be assumed that a resonance adjustment will have been formed simply because of an absence of muscular interference. The real difficulty is that the throat must be maintained in an open position of resonance throughout the duration of the musical phrase. Furthermore, if the singer is to have knowledgeable control over his voice, the resonance adjustment must be volitionally positioned.

The technique for gaining volitional control over involutary movements has already been discussed. By approaching the problem in the manner described, the idea of a volitional positioning of the vocal organs becomes acceptable as a physical and conceptual possibility. On this basis, the singer can sense the nature of involuntary movements and understand how to assist them; he becomes aware of a control potential which avoids the arbitrary and promotes that which is natural. Yet, however skillful the teacher or responsive the pupil, the picture is not complete. What is required now is something extra, and this extra something is the singer's instinct for oral expression. Unless there is a strong desire to break through and fulfill a functional potential, the singer will never experience a truly open-throated resonance adjustment.

Apart from these considerations, the key to open-throated resonance lies with the attack, for it is that which occurs at the moment of tonal inception which will determine the success or failure of a vocal exercise. We have already stressed the need for a rhythmic launching of the phrase, and it has also been emphasized that it is the chest register which serves to dislodge constricting tensions. It is equally important to recall that the register balance must be permitted to readjust for every pitch and intensity, while at the same time the resonance adjustment remains unchanged. All exercises designed to open the throat, therefore, must combine these elements, all of which must be summed up in the attack. Care must also be taken to ensure that the pitch, the vowel, the intensity, and the register balance are all precisely articulated. There must be no slurring; the chest register must be well-coordinated, solid, and secure, and the singer must concentrate on a pure legato. Whatever the shape of the exercise, and for whatever purpose it is employed, if these details are attended to, the throat will not only open, it will remain open.

Another phase of technique which has a direct bearing on open-throated resonance is the factor of tonal duration. In a legato phrase, tonal vitality must be sustained. If tone is not to alter or diminish, the resonance adjustment must not only be formed, it must be maintained. To be precise, it must be 'held.' This need is often recognized, but usually such a holding action is attributed to 'support,' and few methods now in vogue fail to incorporate a special technique of breathing with tonal support as the direct object of instruction.

All methods of breath control have proved to be impractical. Neither the breath nor any technique of controlled breathing is capable of supporting a tone. Acoustically, tone is nothing more than rapidly contracting and expanding air particles, and it is not possible to support moving currents of air. Physically, muscles can either relax or contract, and the kind of relaxation or tension shared by muscles which are mutual antagonists determines the character and efficiency of the coordinative process, not breath support. Support is probably confused with the positioning process which reflects an open-throated resonance adjustment.

A concept somewhat awkward to comprehend here is the use of the word 'held.' But this is precisely what happens! As the vocal organs move reflexly into position to establish a condition of cavity resonance, they must, as long as tonal duration remains a factor, 'hold' the position to assure uniformity of quality. This holding process which maintains the resonance adjustment is crucial, for if it is not correct, in all likelihood the throat will constrict.

If we equate this concept of holding a resonance adjustment with energy output, a better perspective is gained. Energy must, if it is to be utilized economically, be confronted by resistance. This resistence is supplied by the muscles which position the vocal organs. When properly adjusted, all of the laryngeal muscles which function antagonistically are brought into equalized tension and counterbalance one another. When such a balance of tension occurs, the system is said to be in equilibrium. A resonance adjustment, therefore, must literally be 'held' in balanced tension in order to resist the energy output. To the degree that it is maintained in a state of perfect equilibrium, the coordinative process will be correct.

A basic law of physics is applicable to the functional activity here described. It states that 'for every action there is an equal and opposite reaction.' The singer who enjoys a technique where the resonance adjustment and the registration are both held in a condition of balanced tension fulfills that law. his voice will be free because the energy used will prompt a physical *reaction* which will virtually cancel the *action*. As a result, energy is never wasted or diffused.

One may conclude from the foregoing that the establishment of balanced tension is a prerequisite to a secure vocal technique. Such a condition depends upon two factors: 1) registration, which when correctly balanced will cause the edges of the vocal cords to run parallel, thus closing the glottal space, and, 2) open-throated resonance, in which all constrictor tensions caused by muscular interference are absent, thereby opening up unlimited possibilities for accurate 'tuning' of the resonators as a coordinate act with registration.

There is an expression frequently used by the early Italian masters clearly indicating a need for 'holding' (without tenseness) a resonance adjustment. Common reference was made to *'appog-giare la voce,'* to 'lean on the voice.' Obviously, there is but one way to safely lean upon anything, and that is to have a resisting force providing an 'equal and opposite reaction.' To accomplish this, the muscles which position the resonators must 'hold.' It is a natural equilibrium among opposing muscle groups which leads a performer into believing his tone to be 'supported.' To attribute this feeling to any special technique of controlled breathing would be a tragic error.

An interesting sidelight of functional training is the physical symptoms which invariably accompany a release of constrictor tension and the consequent opening of the throat. Yawning, dizzi-ness, giggling, tingling sensations, and distracting conversation are common, while quite frequently the student will complain of having to regurgitate. On rare occasions, symptoms of asthma will make it almost impossible for the singer to phonate, a symptom which always accompanies an obviously more open-throated condition of resonance. Another oddity is the singer's tendency to stop in the midst of a tone which is undeniably freer. In such instances, it is difficult to judge whether the interruption is due to being ill at ease with a new tonal identity, or whether it grows out of anxiety. Quite clearly, contact with natural movement leads to sensual awareness and a breakdown of psychic defenses.

Muscular movements made in agreement with functional logic are impossible unless constrictor tensions due to poor physical co-ordination and/or emotional repression have been eliminated. If the vocal mechanism is to work properly, both psychic and physi-cal energy must be discharged adequately and economically. Throat constriction and a mixed registration dissipate energy and must be cured if the vocal technique is to be free.

REFERENCES

1. Baker, Elsworth F.: *Man in the Trap.* New York: Macmillan Company, 1967, pp. 4 and 29.

2. Clippenger, D. A.: *The Head Voice and Other Problems.* Boston, Mass.: Oliver Ditson & Company, 1917, p. 30.

3. Macini, G.: *Practical Reflections on Figured Singing,* translated by E. Forman. Champaign, Illinois: Pro Musica Press, 1967, p. 115.

4. Nathan, Isaac: *Musurgia Vocalis.* London, England: Fentum, 1836, p. 117 and 118.

5. Lehmann, Lilli: *How to Sing,* translated by Richard Aldrich. New York: The Macmillan Company, 1910.

6. Bonci, Alessandro: *The Daily Mail.* London, June 30, 1908.

7. Klein, Herman: *The Bel Canto.* London: Oxford University Press, 1923, p. 20.

8. Garcia, Manuel: *Hints on Singing.* New York: Edw. Schuberth & Company, Inc., 1894, pp. 12 ,40.

9. Marafioti, P. M.: *Caruso's Method of Voice Production.* New York: Appleton-Century Company, 1937, p. 69.

10. Appleman, D. Ralph: *Science of Vocal Pedagogy.* Bloomington, Ind.: Indiana University Press, 1967, p. 231.

11. Vennard, William: *Singing: The Mechanism & Technique.* New York: Carl Fischer, Inc., 1967, pp. 94, 157.

12. Tosi, Pier. F.: *Observations on the Florid Song,* translated by Galliard. London: Reeves Bookseller, Ltd., Reprinted 1926, pp. 18 and 25.

13. Witherspoon, H.: *Singing.* New York: G. Schirmer, 1945, pp. 21, 35. IBID: *A Treatise for Teachers and Students.* New York: G. Schirmer, Inc., 1925, p. 23.

14. Curtis, H. H.: *Voice Building & Tone Placing.* New York: Appleton & Company, 1900, p. 160.

15. White, E. G.: *Sinus Tone Production.* London: J. M. Dent and Sons, 1938, pp. 8, 90, 91, & 94.

16. Wooldridge, Warren B.: *Doctoral Dissertation Series,* University Microfilm, Ann Arbor, Michigan: Pub. No. 10, 161; Indiana University, 1954.

17. Howard, John.: *The Physiology of Artistic Singing.* New York, 1886.

18. Brown, Wm. E.: *Vocal Wisdom, or The Maxims of J. B. Lamperti.* Brooklyn, New York, Distributed: L. Strongin, p. 69.

19. Shakespeare, Wm.: *The Art of Singing.* Bryn-Mawr, Penn.: Theodore Presser Company, 1921, p. 27.

20. Husler, Frederick & Yvonne Rodd-Marling: *Singing: The Physical Nature of the Vocal Organ.* New York: October House, Inc., 1965, p. 25.

21. Reich, Wilhelm: *Selected Writings.* New York: Farrar, Straus & Cudahy, 1960, p. 148.

22. Mancini, G. B.: *Practical Reflections on the Figurative Art of Singing,* Milan, 1776, translated by Pietro Buzzi. Boston, Mass.: The Gorham Press, 1912.

23. Tenducci, G. F.: *Instruction of Mr. Tenducci to His Scholars.* London: Longman & Broderip, c.a. 1785.

24. Lamperti, F.: *A Treatise on the Art of Singing,* translated by J. C. Griffith. New York: G. Schirmer & Co., 1877.

25. Lindsley, C. F.: *Psycho-Physical Determinants of Individual Differences in Voice Quality.* Los Angeles, California, Unpublished Dissertation, PhD., University of Southern California, 1932. (Reference obtained from William Vennard's book, *Singing: the Mechanism and the Technique.*)

BIBLIOGRAPHY

APPLEMAN, D. RALPH: *The Science of Vocal Pedagogy.* Bloomington: Indiana University Press, 1967.

BARTHOLOMEW, WILMER T.: *Acoustics of Music.* New York: Prentice Hall, Inc., 1942.

BEHNKE, E.: *The Mechanism of the Human Voice.* London: J. Curwen & Sons, 1880.

BROWN, LENNOX, AND BEHNKE: *Voice, Song and Speech.* New York: G. P. Putnam's Sons, (circa 1890).

FLETCHER, HARVEY: *Speech and Hearing.* New York: Van Nostrand, 1929.

HUSLER, FREDERICK and YVONNE RODD-MARLING: *Singing: The Physical Nature of the Vocal Organ.* London: Faber and Faber, Ltd., 1965.

MACKENZI, SIR MORRELL: *Hygiene of the Vocal Organs,* Belmar, New Jersey: Edgar S. Werner & Company, Ninth Edition, 1928 (First Edition, circa 1887).

MOSES, PAUL J.: *The Voice of Neurosis.* New York: Grune & Stratton, 1954.

NEGUS, VICTOR E.: *The Mechanism of the Larynx.* London: Wm. Heineman, Ltd., 1929.

REDFIELD, JOHN: *Music: A Science and an Art.* New York: Tudor Publishing Company, 1926.

ROSE, ARNOLD: *The Singer and the Voice.* London: Faber and Faber, Ltd., 1962.

SEASHORE, CARL: *Psychology of Music.* New York: McGraw-Hill Book Company, Inc., 1938.

SCRIPTURE, E. W.: *Researches in Experimental Phonetics.* Washington, D. C.: Carnegie Institution, 1906.

STANLEY, DOUGLAS: *The Science of Voice.* New York: Carl Fischer, Inc., 1929.

149

ARTICLES

DEW, ROBERT A., M.D.: "The Biopathic Diathesis" (Part V: An Introduction to the Pulmonary Biopathies), *Journal of Orgonomy*, Vol. 6: No. 1, May 1972.

PRESSMAN, JOEL J.: "Physiology of the Vocal Cords in Phonation and Respiration", *Arch. Otolaryng*, 35: 1942.

VAN DE BERG and J. T. ZANTEMA and P. DOORNENBAL: "On the Air Resistance and the Bernoulli Effect of the Human Larynx": *Journal Acoust. Soc. of America*, 29: 1957.

VENNARD, WILLIAM: "An Experiment to Evaluate the Importance of Nasal Resonance in Singing": *Folia Phoniat.*, 16: 1964.

WOLFE, THEODORE P., M.D.: "The Sex-Economic Concept of Psychosomatic Identity and Antithesis": New York, *Journal of Orgonomy*, Vol. 4, No. 1, May 1970.

ZERFFI, W. A. C.: "Laryngology and Voice Production": *Annal. Oto. Rhin. and Laryng.*, 61, 1952.

NOTES

NOTES

NOTES

NOTES